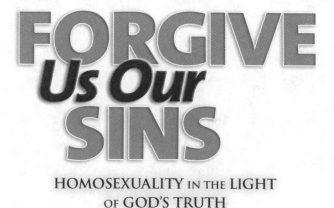

FORGIVE Us Our SINS

HOMOSEXUALITY in the LIGHT of GOD'S TRUTH

Scott I. Barefoot and Richard D. Starr

NORTHWESTERN PUBLISHING HOUSE

Milwaukee, Wisconsin

Third printing,   2015
Second printing, 2014

Photo: Shutterstock
Art Director: Karen Knutson
Designer: Pamela Dunn

Northwestern Publishing House
1250 N. 113th St. Milwaukee, WI 53226-3284
www.nph.net
© 2013 by Northwestern Publishing House
Published 2013
Printed in the United States of America
ISBN 978-0-8100-2595-0
ISBN 978-0-8100-2596-7(e-book)

CONTENTS

Introduction v

CHAPTER ONE Why a Book on Homosexuality? 1

CHAPTER TWO The Cause 12

CHAPTER THREE The Word of God—Old Testament 24

CHAPTER FOUR The Word of God—New Testament 34

CHAPTER FIVE The Change 56

CHAPTER SIX The Support 75

Endnotes 91

INTRODUCTION

In 1983, when I first wrote a paper on the topic of homosexuality, I was a young pastor trying to start a home mission in northwest Columbus, Ohio. I had had my first encounter with an actively gay man who was interested in joining my mission church but was not interested in leaving the gay lifestyle. As I sought help for dealing with that particular situation, I found there was precious little in our circles written on the topic. In fact, there were very few written resources on the subject at all that were true to Scripture. Then I, together with about 250 other participants, attended a seminar on human sexuality at a local Lutheran seminary, hoping for some insight. An elderly African-American Baptist minister, an older Roman Catholic nun, and I were the only three participants at the seminar who stood up for what the Bible says on the subject of practicing homosexuality. I realized then that I was not going to get any help from outside sources.

I suggested to the steering committee of my pastoral conference that someone should write a paper on the subject of homosexuality. I reasoned that we hadn't had much instruction at the seminary on how to deal with those trapped in that sin, and it was painfully obvious to me that we were going to be dealing with that sin more and more. The committee assigned the paper to me.

After I delivered the paper at a meeting of the conference, my pastoral colleagues kindly suggested that it should be sent to Wisconsin Lutheran Seminary to be available in the library so that other pastors might benefit from it. They also resolved that the conference should send the paper to Northwestern Publishing House for consideration as a book.

Northwestern Publishing House requested that I expand the paper and write it for a general audience, not just for pastors. In 1987, *Speaking the Unspeakable: Homosexuality—A Biblical and Modern*

Perspective was published by Northwestern Publishing House. Eventually the book went out of print. However, over the years I continued to receive requests for a copy of the book or for advice on how to deal with a situation involving a gay parishioner, family member, or friend.

A few years ago, the Wisconsin Evangelical Lutheran Synod Conference of Presidents requested that I write a Bible study on the topic of homosexuality. That Bible study, *Deadly Desires*, was published by Northwestern Publishing House in 2008. It includes student lessons, a leader's guide, and a PowerPoint presentation for each lesson, all on a CD. At the time of this writing, it is still available from Northwestern Publishing House.

During the time I was writing the Bible study, a young man from Virginia, Scott Barefoot, contacted me. He had been given a copy of *Speaking the Unspeakable* by a pastor, and after reading it, he wanted to thank me for helping him put so much of his life in perspective with God's Word. Through numerous telephone conversations and e-mails, Scott shared his life story with me.

As I completed each lesson of the Bible study *Deadly Desires*, I field-tested it at my own congregation in Bay City, Michigan, and also shared it with Scott. He was excited about the Bible study because he saw in it exactly what is needed for dealing with the sin of homosexuality (or any sin, for that matter). God's law is presented clearly and emphatically, leaving no room for "spin" by so-called gay Christians. God's gospel is presented with love and compassion, giving the motivation and the power for change. Eventually Scott himself presented that Bible study to a group of Christians in his area.

For some time, Northwestern Publishing House has wanted me to write an update of *Speaking the Unspeakable*. My long-suffering editor, Ray Schumacher, has had tremendous patience with me in completing the task. I had found the assignment difficult to carry out because I really didn't feel that there was anything new to be said on the subject. Yes, society and other Christian churches have become more tolerant, accepting, and supportive of homosexuality. However, the way to deal with that has not changed, because God's

Word does not change. Therefore, what I had written in *Speaking the Unspeakable* had not changed. I needed to find a new approach.

That is where my friend Scott Barefoot fulfilled a need. He was willing to share his life's journey into and out of the gay lifestyle. He would do so in six installments. Each installment would correspond to a chapter in the book. After each installment of Scott's journey, I would elaborate on a lesson from the Bible study *Deadly Desires* and apply the Word of God to that part of Scott's journey. In addition to teaching the Bible study in Virginia, Scott also made several presentations about his journey out of the gay lifestyle to pastors and lay leaders in Wisconsin and Michigan. Scott wrote a feature article on the subject for *Forward in Christ,* a monthly periodical of the Wisconsin Evangelical Lutheran Synod. These were extremely courageous efforts on his part. The book you are holding in your hand is the result of our combined efforts.

It is our most sincere desire and prayer that if you are struggling with the temptation of practicing homosexuality, you will find Scott's journey inspiring as you receive power through the Word of God to overcome that temptation. If you are a relative, friend, or fellow church family member of someone struggling with or trapped in homosexuality, it is our most sincere desire and prayer that this book will help you find God-pleasing ways to help that person overcome the temptation or to leave the gay lifestyle.

Please note that while you will find very practical advice, both from someone who has personally lived through the struggle and from a parish pastor trained in the original languages of the Bible, you will not find a quick and easy cure-all, silver bullet, or magic formula to "cure" homosexuality. There is no cure for homosexuality other than the one cure for any and all sin: Holy Spirit-worked faith in the forgiveness of our Savior Jesus Christ.

God bless your use of this book.

—*Pastor Richard D. Starr,*
redeemed child of God

CHAPTER ONE

WHY A BOOK
ON HOMOSEXUALITY?

SCOTT'S JOURNEY
Part 1: The Slippery Slope to "the Fall"

I grew up during the 1980s in what is considered rural northern Virginia, a place called Fauquier County. It's "horse country," about 60 miles southwest of Washington, DC. While it is so close to the "big city," to my way of thinking it was still pretty far removed from it and very much a small town. My family and I had to drive 30 to 40 minutes to get to church, the nearest shopping mall, movie theatres, etc.

By all accounts I had a very sheltered upbringing. I was baptized as an infant in a local Lutheran Church—Missouri Synod congregation, and years later I was confirmed in the local Wisconsin Evangelical Lutheran Synod church. Back then there was no such thing as the Internet, or even affordable home personal computers. (In fact, I was one of the first proud owners of an Atari video game system.)

From as far back as I can remember, but especially in junior and senior high school, I was always in awe of the good-looking guys in my school. I consciously tried to befriend them, tried to emulate them, and spent most of my time and effort trying to get close to them. The odd thing was, while I was always a bit self-consciously awkward, I was considered by many girls to be a good catch with my blond hair, blue eyes, and decent looks. Back then there was no physical or sexual component to my feelings about other boys. There was just a desire to be part of the "in crowd" with the rest of the guys. At the outset, I don't think my feelings and desires were much different from those of other boys my age.

As I progressed through high school, I recognized that the other boys' attentions had begun to turn toward girls. It became a badge of honor

1

to date one cute girl or another. I remember that that wasn't as important to me. I continued to just enjoy and seek the companionship and friendship of the good-looking and popular guys, the ones I had always sought friendship with.

By the time I reached my junior, and especially my senior, year of high school, I began to sense that there was "trouble in River City." Most guys were either dating or actively seeking to date girls. GIRLS? I continued to have absolutely no physical attraction to girls. I found them to be great friends, but friends were all I had ever considered them to be. I never had any thoughts like, Wow, I'd really like to date or get to first base with that girl!

Instead I began to think such things as, What would it be like to get to first base with my friend Mike? *However, there was never a conscious point at which I thought,* I don't feel an attraction to girls. I'd rather be attracted to and pursue guys instead. *That never occurred.*

This is difficult for me to explain to male acquaintances who grew up feeling an automatic attraction to girls. It's not something they ever had to think about. It just was. It happened. It was second nature for them. That was never the case for me.

As I began to connect the dots about my sexuality, I knew my feelings and attractions were different from most and that they seemed to be more focused on other guys. I knew there were people who were said to be "gay." But other than hearing in church that being gay was a sin, I didn't know a whole lot about that subculture. Growing up out in the country as I did, about the only exposure I had to gay people was the news coverage about the annual gay pride events in Washington, DC. Of course, when it came to that sort of television coverage, I only saw pictures and images of the most outrageous looking and outrageously dressed people in gay pride parades. These were the guys dressed as women or wearing obnoxious outfits—barely clad, wearing leather gear, tattooed and pierced, etc.

Growing up in the WELS (Wisconsin Evangelical Lutheran Synod), a church body that faithfully teaches and practices God's Word, I knew very well what God says about homosexuality. But I believed I couldn't resist having these sinful attractions and feelings.

In high school my feelings indirectly affected my social interactions. I immersed myself in extracurricular activities such as the marching band. At the age of 15, I volunteered for my hometown rescue squad. I attended night vocational classes and, by the time I was 16, obtained my emergency medical technician certification. Other kids my age were heavily into the high school social scene and were hanging out together after school, attending parties, dating, and so on. But I skipped all of that. Instead, most days after school and most Friday and Saturday nights, I'd head over to the rescue squad.

I think there were a couple of reasons for this. The first was that I knew I was different in my feelings and attractions and didn't really fit in with the regular high school social scene. Working was sort of an excuse for me. When invited to parties, to go to movies, to just hang out, etc., I had a ready-made and legitimate excuse not to participate: I had commitments at the rescue squad. Also, in the back of my mind, I knew my thoughts and attractions were not God-pleasing. So, with warped rationalization I believed I could balance out the bad by immersing myself in good, that is, volunteering my time to help my fellow man. What more noble and good activity could I have chosen to become involved in? I'm sure most parents of teenagers would love to have their teenager involved in such activities instead of becoming involved in some of the idle mischief that many teenagers get into.

Then it was off to college. I was accepted by and opted to attend George Mason University (GMU) in Fairfax, Virginia. Even though GMU wasn't more than a 40-minute drive from my home, I got my parents to agree to pay for me to live on campus. I very easily could have commuted to and from college classes, but I wanted to get the "full college experience." And probably even more important to me—some FREEDOM!

This was really where my slide into embracing the sin of homosexuality took off. I took advantage of the liberal college campus life to further investigate homosexuality. I remember that there was actually a Gay and Lesbian Student Alliance club that met regularly on campus in one of the student unions. While I never had the nerve to actually attend one of the meetings, I recall sort of casing the meetings. I would make a point to linger in the student union, in the vicinity of the meetings,

3

so I could get a glimpse of some of the folks who were attending. I was curious to see and possibly meet someone who was openly gay. To my disappointment, the group's meetings were sparsely attended (probably no more than five or six people attended—maybe five very masculine lesbians and one very oddly dressed and extremely effeminate guy). So I quickly gave up on that avenue.

As it turned out, I came into contact with an RA (dormitory resident advisor) named Eric, whose room was next to mine. He was a very handsome looking and masculine guy. Our paths happened to cross multiple times in the course of a typical week on campus. I remember he had piercing blue eyes that rivaled my own, and we often found ourselves maintaining eye contact for much longer than two straight guys normally would. Being an RA, he was an upperclassman, and I was, of course, a lowly freshman. One day when I was in the library, he made a point of coming over and sitting beside me at a table while I was studying. He introduced himself to me and started making small talk. I remember that my heart started racing and I was filled with an indescribable excitement. I couldn't begin to tell you what we talked about, but we both rambled on for hours. While the conversation itself was forgettable, I do remember that our eye contact never broke during this time. That seems to be where it began. For those of you who have never experienced homosexual tendencies, if you want to try to relate, just substitute one of your first high school or college "crushes" of the opposite sex for this guy, Eric. That was what it was like for me.

After that meeting Eric and I quickly became best friends. We'd always make a point of eating meals together and studying at the library together. These were typical friend activities, but all the while there was this distinctive and mutual below-the-surface physical attraction. I can't adequately describe it in words, but there was just a mutual feeling (as he'd later admit to me) that there was more between us than just a regular guy-guy friendship.

Allow me to interject a few words about what was going on in my spiritual life. From the time I entered college, I subconsciously began to distance myself from God and the church. One of the freedoms that I began to take advantage of was the freedom from parental control. I found convenient reasons for skipping church on a regular basis.

At the time, I saw God and church as something I was required to participate in by my parents while living at home. Of course, subconsciously, attending church and hearing God's Word were the source of my feelings of guilt when it came to my attractions to other guys. The less I attended church, the less "dirty" I felt about having these attractions.

This led to what eventually happened with Eric and me. After months of close friendship, he invited me to go home with him for a weekend when his parents were out of town. That was the point where our friendship progressed to physical intimacy. I found it both exhilarating and "dirty" at the same time. This is where I really have a tough time putting my experience into words, but I believe it is important. I've long felt and said that throughout the decade when I was living that sinful lifestyle, I always had a sense in the back of my mind that what I was doing was a sin. This first sexual experience with Eric was typical of every subsequent sexual encounter I'd have with other guys. There was this exhilaration and profound physical arousal leading up to the sexual act. But then after the climax, I couldn't help but feel an extreme letdown and sense of shame.

After that sexual experience with Eric, he and I distanced ourselves from each other. We went back to school and never again looked at each other in the same way. We never spoke of the incident.

Some would say, "Well, you did it once and it didn't turn out the way you thought, so it should have been easy at that point for you to stop." Well, that's easier said than done.

After college when I was truly out on my own—working a full-time job, living on my own, and supporting myself—I reached the point where those physical yearnings for other guys began to take over again. This time I started searching out places where adult gay people met and congregated. I searched for and found the hub of the gay community in Washington, DC. When I talk about the hub, I'm referring to the bars and restaurants where gay people meet and congregate in public.

There I found my eyes pleasantly opened. I've mentioned how turned-off I was at the sight of some of the people in the news coverage of the gay pride parades and other events. To my amazement, when I had *the courage to venture into the city to one of those gay bars, I found myself surrounded by hundreds of good-looking, run-of-the-mill, masculine-acting guys like myself! I was shocked that the extremely effeminate looking and acting guys actually made up a very small minority of the guys that I saw at this gay bar. Wow! Here were other gay guys that I could actually relate to! These were guys like myself. If I had seen them walking down the street or in a shopping mall, I would have had no clue they were gay. That was it for me; I was hooked. I became even more blown away when one of the guys I met at this gay bar invited me to visit his church, where other gay people went and where the pastor himself was gay! I was in utter shock and amazement. Was it possible that I had been duped all of those years growing up? Could it be that God really has no condemnation for homosexuality after all? Were these feelings of guilt I had experienced all those years completely misplaced?*

A TIMELY TOPIC

"Why a book on homosexuality? Isn't it a cut-and-dried issue in the Scriptures? Besides, homosexuality deals with a very small portion of society. Certainly no one I know would ever be involved in such a thing!" said a longtime member of the church, uncomfortable with even discussing the topic.

"I need help with these desires I'm experiencing. For so long I've been sure that no other Christian has such feelings. For so long I've been sure that no other Christian would understand what I feel. For so long I've felt so alone, so confused, so dirty," lamented a member of the church who for years, like Scott, had attended the church's Sunday school, elementary school, and youth group.

"I sure hope this study gives me the answers I need to change the views on homosexuality of my friend/relative/child/spouse. It just breaks my heart to know that he/she thinks being gay is okay. Yet every time I bring up the subject, I'm the one accused of being judgmental, unloving, and non-Christian. Help!" cry concerned Christians looking for answers but erroneously taking on themselves the work of the Holy Spirit.

You may be thinking some of these thoughts. At any rate, for some reason you've picked up this book and have started reading it. It may be out of simple curiosity. It may be that you're just looking for some information on a subject about which you know very little. It may be that you are greatly troubled because of your feelings and actions. Regardless of your motivation, let me ask you a question or two before going any further. Think about your answers carefully and be honest—you are the only one who will know how you answered, but you may not be the only one who will benefit from those answers or from this book.

What would you do if your son or daughter, nephew or niece, or even your spouse suddenly told you that he or she was gay? How would you respond to Scott, whom you just met in the opening pages of this book? Scott is a very real person who is sharing his true story with you. What if Scott were to move next door to you, come to you for counseling, or join your congregation? Would you recoil from him in revulsion, pretend he didn't exist, or even tell him to "get out and stay out" until he changed his ways? Is that what you would do with your son or daughter, nephew or niece, or even your spouse, who confessed to you that he or she was gay?

If you are at all aware of the world around you, you know that all of society is currently affected by homosexuality. There is a relentless full-court press on us not only to tolerate the practice of homosexuality but to accept it as a normal lifestyle. This pressure comes from the media, from unbelievers who want nothing to do with "right-wing Christian morality," and from those who claim to be Christian believers but who want to change God's Word to make it more palatable for our sinful natures, so as not to offend sinners. You can see that this was happening to Scott with disastrous results as he slid further and further down that slippery slope into accepting homosexuality as normal, natural, and acceptable for a practicing Christian. We Christians need to study God's Word to help keep us from becoming desensitized to the sin of practicing homosexuality. That is one of the purposes of this book.

Like Scott, you may be one of those who are struggling every day with desires you know are wrong. You may be tempted to believe all that you hear from society about those desires. You may give in at times to those desires. But after you do, you realize your sin, repent, ask for forgiveness and strength, and receive those blessings. Yet the desires come back and you fall again . . . and again . . . and again. When will it ever end? You may ask, "Why doesn't God take these desires away from me? Why doesn't he help?" One of the purposes of this book is to help you see how God wants to help you every day.

You may be appalled, confused, and frustrated by a friend's or relative's desire to engage in homosexual activity. You may feel helpless, not knowing which way to turn but desperately wanting to help the person. You may think that if you just say the right words, your loved one will see the light and change his or her behavior. Remember that changing a person's heart is the work of the Holy Spirit; we are not equipped to do that. However, there are ways to approach and help a person struggling with the sin of practicing homosexuality. One of the purposes of this book is to help you learn what you can do.

Of course, the church has always been a formidable force in keeping homosexuality in check. But that too is changing. This change is being led by seminary professors and the clergy. "I am a child of God, a man, a homosexual, a Christian, a Lutheran—in that order—and I am a husband committed to my wife, who knows I'm gay." The author of this statement was a 33-year-old Lutheran minister serving a Midwestern parish. Although this pro-homosexual trend is currently changing for many Christians— including Lutherans—by God's grace, such is not the case for the Wisconsin Evangelical Lutheran Synod.

Homosexuality is a subject that demands the attention of every concerned Bible-believing person today. It won't simply go away, and it would be wrong (although convenient) to ignore it. We all must be prepared to respond in an appropriate and Christian manner to the person, like Scott, caught in the sin of homosexuality.

DEFINING HOMOSEXUALITY

The dictionary defines *homosexual* in this way: "of, relating to, or exhibiting sexual desire toward a member of one's own sex." For our purposes, we will add *behavior* in addition to *desire*. *Homosexuality* refers to overt sexual relations or emotional attachment involving sexual attraction between individuals—male or female—of the same sex. Certainly *homosexual* does not describe a person's physical appearance or mannerisms. Effeminate traits in a man or masculine traits in a woman do not identify either as homosexual. Scott explained how he was actually turned off by guys who displayed effeminate characteristics, but was greatly attracted to masculine guys who looked and acted straight. He was surprised and pleased to learn that there were gay guys, like him, who did not appear gay to others.

We know that God did not create Adam and Eve to be homosexual. God's plan is for human beings to be heterosexual. He created Adam and Eve, not Adam and Steve. We read in Genesis 2:24, "For this reason a man will leave his father and mother and be united to his wife, and they will become one flesh." The sin of homosexuality has undoubtedly been present in this world for a very long time. It can be found in the history of almost every land and culture. While sin has been with us since the fall and the sin of homosexuality has been with us since early on—it was not from the very start of things. After his work of creation, "God saw all that he had made, and it was very good" (Genesis 1:31). God does not consider homosexuality "very good."

In the following Bible passages, God tells us exactly how he feels about homosexuality. In Leviticus 18:22,24 God says, "Do not lie with a man as one lies with a woman; that is detestable. Do not defile yourselves in any of these ways, because this is how the nations that I am going to drive out before you became defiled." Later in Leviticus 20:13 God says, "If a man lies with a man as one lies with a woman, both of them have done what is detestable. They must be put to death; their blood will be on their own heads." The New Testament is just as clear and straightforward in its blanket condemnation of the sin of homosexuality. We read in Romans 1:26,27, "Because of this, God gave them over to shameful lusts. Even their women exchanged natural relations for unnatural ones. In the same way the men also abandoned natural relations with women and were inflamed with lust for one another. Men committed indecent acts with other men, and received in themselves the due penalty for their perversion." This passage speaks explicitly against both lesbianism and homosexuality. Homosexuality is listed among other damning sins in 1 Corinthians 6:9,10: "Do you not know that the wicked will not inherit the kingdom of God? Do not be deceived: Neither the sexually immoral nor idolaters nor adulterers nor male prostitutes nor homosexual offenders nor thieves nor the greedy nor drunkards nor slanderers nor swindlers will inherit the kingdom of God." In all these passages, God teaches us that homosexuality is a sin—and God hates all sin. He also warns, in very strong terms, that anyone who persists in the practice of homosexuality is under his condemnation. Of course, this is true of anyone who persists in any unrepented sin. This is the truth that must be proclaimed to every unrepentant sinner.

When you read Scott's account of his fall into living the sinful lifestyle of a practicing homosexual, you can feel his conflict and anguish. He knew what he was doing was wrong. He was attracted to it and then repulsed by it. He didn't understand the desires, but he knew they were there and he knew he had acted on them. The apostle Paul understood that conflict and anguish over sin. He wrote about his personal struggles with overcoming sin, both sinful desires and behavior:

> I do not understand what I do. For what I want to do I do not do, but what I hate I do. And if I do what I do not want to do, I agree that the law is good. As it is, it is no longer I myself who do it, but it is sin living in me. I know that nothing good lives in me, that is, in my sinful nature. For I have the desire to do what is good, but I cannot carry it out. For what I do is not the good I want to do; no, the evil I do not want to do—this I keep on doing. Now if I do what I do not want to do, it is no longer I who do it, but it is sin living in me that does it. So I find this law at work: When I want to do good, evil is right there with me. For in my inner being I delight in God's law; but I see another law at work in the members of my body, waging war against the law of my mind and making me a prisoner of the law of sin at work within my members. What a wretched man I am! Who will rescue me from this body of death? (Romans 7:15-24)

St. Paul struggled mightily with conflicting desires because he was, as Luther was fond of saying, both sinner and saint. So is every Christian. Every Christian experiences the conflict between the desire to do God's will and the desire to satisfy his or her own flesh. The Christian who is struggling with homosexuality, like Scott, knows this struggle all too well. However, today that struggling Christian is being told, even by churches, that he or she does not need to struggle with the sin of homosexuality, that being gay is "natural" and "normal." Recall the church Scott was invited to attend, which was served by an openly gay pastor. Churches are telling gays that they can live a God-pleasing life and still practice homosexuality. As we have seen, this is in direct contradiction of God's clear Word.

In light of St. Paul's struggle with conflicting desires and our own struggles with the temptation to sin, we should offer loving counsel and support to the person who is struggling with homosexual desires. That does not mean we condone sin or offer excuses for it. However, far too often the church and Christians have offered only condemnation and rejection instead of help and support to brothers and sisters who struggle against and sometimes fall into the sin of homosexuality. This is due to the fact that for most people, homosexuality is an unnatural sin (Romans 1:26,27). For most people, this is a desire with which they cannot identify because they are not tempted by it. The sin of homosexuality is not "natural"; it is "unnatural." For that reason, many Christians are more repulsed by that sin than, for example, the sins of adultery and gossip; sins with which they have been tempted and for which they may feel more empathy.

You may not be tempted by the sin of homosexuality. Thank God for that blessing! But all sin damns, and as St. Paul stated so beautifully, there is only one solution for sin: "Thanks be to God—through Jesus Christ our Lord!" (Romans 7:25). St. Paul found strength for his struggle with conflicting desires in Jesus Christ our Lord. We, and all Christians struggling with deadly desires—including Scott—find our forgiveness, our comfort, and our strength only in our Savior Jesus Christ.

CHAPTER TWO

THE CAUSE

SCOTT'S JOURNEY
Part 2: Descending Further—Coming Out

In my early twenties, I fell headlong into living a life of sinful sexual immorality in the form of homosexuality. I had begun dating guys and engaging in sexual relations with them. To a large degree I was blinded to my sin at that time because I surrounded myself with others like me. As I mentioned, I experienced what felt at the time to be an amazingly wonderful discovery: openly gay guys. They seemed to be normal guys like myself. I felt understood by others for the first time in a long time. I felt relieved I could now "be myself" around other people. As I became a more active participant in the gay community, I met more gay Christians and gay spiritual leaders. Now, looking back, I can see that those people were nothing more than wolves in sheep's clothing (Matthew 7:15).

Even in the secular world at that time (early 1990s), many "experts," both medical researchers and psychologists, were contending that people were born homosexual or gay. They were supposedly on the verge of isolating and producing concrete genetic proof of this. There was supposedly some evidence that a homosexual's brain, when compared to that of a heterosexual, was visibly different. The American Board of Psychiatry even issued what I believe was an official position on homosexuality. Basically, it stated that it was tantamount to malpractice to try to treat or cure someone for just being a homosexual.

For centuries, most gay people lived their lives "in the closet." They lived in fear of persecution by society. The 1990s saw the beginning of a trend of tolerance and acceptance as people, even some famous celebrities, came "out of the closet" in large numbers. The gay rights movement really began to solidify and take off. The push for governments (local, state, and national) to enact legislation to prohibit discrimination based on a person's sexual orientation began to succeed.

I had found camaraderie, friendship, and acceptance in the gay community. And at the same time, I saw the world around me starting to legitimize homosexuality. One could look back at the timing of all of this in conjunction with the continued distancing of myself from God as the brewing of a perfect storm in my life.

When many of my new acquaintances and friends heard of my conservative Lutheran and Christian upbringing, they offered their condolences to me. They encouraged me to be thankful for finally seeing the light and accepting that it was okay to be gay.

I quickly became well versed in all the spin and talking points of the gay community. I could and did recite the following:

- *"I never chose to be gay; I was born this way."*

- *"From as far back as I can remember, I've always been attracted to guys."*

- *"Who would actually choose to be gay? If it were actually a choice, I would've chosen to be heterosexual. My life would be so much easier."*

- *"I believe God created certain people to be gay. Why would he do that, if it were a sin?"*

- *"What would you do if you woke up tomorrow in a world where homosexuality was considered the norm but all you felt was an attraction to the opposite sex?"*

By so completely submersing in and surrounding myself with this positive reinforcement of sin and homosexuality, I eventually became emboldened enough to "come out" to my family and friends. I'll preface this by saying that for several years prior to this, I had distanced myself from my family as well as the church and the true Word of God.

I started my journey of coming out to people by first sharing the news with some of my past non-Christian friends. They were mostly past and current coworkers and acquaintances, who seemed pretty laid-back in general. Not surprisingly, many were very supportive of my news and revelation. My gay friends continued to cheer me on in these endeavors. They told me flat out that if I encountered people who couldn't accept the fact I was gay, then it was their issue, not mine. After coming out to friends, the next logical step, I felt, was to have "the talk" with my parents.

I'll never forget the evening I decided to come out to my parents. I had called them, stating that I'd like to come over for dinner because I had something I wanted to tell them. I remember being so nervous and preoccupied with the announcement I had gone there to make that it seemed like dinner lasted forever. After dinner my folks and I went into the living room alone. I was now in the spotlight. They sat anxiously, waiting to hear my news.

Before I could even start to get the words out, I broke into tears. Then I managed to blurt it out all at once: "Mom and Dad, I'm gay." I went on to explain how I'd had the feelings for years, felt that I was born that way, and so on. Looking back now, I can see that all the torment and emotional upheaval I went through as I revealed my feelings should have raised more red flags in my mind. But back then I felt as if I were removing a huge burden from my shoulders. I may have felt that a burden had been removed from me, but as they later shared with me, my parents felt that they had become the recipients of a new burden.

I remember that my dad just sat there in complete and solemn silence. My mom was actually the first to break the silence, with this surprising statement: "I think I've probably always known this." After that, things became somewhat bizarre and hazy. My mother seemed curiously inquisitive, wanting to know things like when I first began experimenting, with whom, and so on. Then I vaguely recall my dad eventually voicing his disbelief and disapproval. He didn't want to hear or say anything further about it that night. I can honestly say that, even to this day, my relationship with my parents has never been quite what it was before that fateful night.

Over the coming weeks, my dad began to speak to me more and share both his feelings and God's law very explicitly. I received more than a couple long, multipage letters from him, full of Scripture and repeated appeals for me to change and repent.

Eventually, I reluctantly agreed to meet with the WELS pastor at the church where I had been confirmed and where my parents were still active members. The pastor there was very young. He was actually not much older than I at the time, in his midtwenties. I remember he received the call, or assignment, to come to that congregation directly from Wisconsin Lutheran Seminary.

I called and made an appointment to meet with him. I remember doing this, more or less, to appease my dad. I did not think my heart was open to the possibility of changing. When I called, I didn't explain the reason I wanted to meet. I assumed that my parents had probably already filled him in.

It did end up being a very memorable meeting. As I indicated earlier, I really hadn't attended church there very regularly for quite awhile. I remember sitting across from the desk in the pastor's office. As I had done with my parents, I just basically blurted out that I had come to the realization that I was gay. I'll never quite forget the sight, watching the color drain from his face as I went on to share the rest of what I had gone over with my parents. I remember sitting through a period of awkward silence, after which he said that the seminary hadn't really prepared him for this type of counseling. He did pull out his Bible and read some of the passages that my dad had shared with me in his correspondence over the past few weeks.

In a way, I had felt a great deal of guilt for not telling my parents and others earlier. Prior to that I obviously had to edit out quite a bit of my life when I talked with certain friends and family members. Now, in a warped way, I felt like I had done them and me a favor by coming out. I no longer had to be deceitful about how I was living my life. If they couldn't accept it, it was now their problem and issue, not mine.

But by coming out, I had sunk even further into that lifestyle and cycle of unrepented sin.

THE CAUSE OF HOMOSEXUALITY

Could you sense the anxiety and tension Scott felt as he contemplated and carried out this important step? Scott felt anxious and tense because even though he was denying it at the time, in his heart he knew he was sinning. He was embracing a sinful lifestyle, and he was asking his parents to condone that sin by accepting him as a homosexual. After coming out to his parents, Scott felt relief. In part, that was the relief of a confessed sin. King David knew that feeling. In Psalm 32:3 he wrote, "When I kept silent, my bones wasted away through my groaning all day long." However, Scott's relief would not last because although he had confessed his sin, he had not repented of it. The devil, Scott's gay friends, and Scott's own sinful nature had convinced him that his homosexual behavior was not sinful, so there was no reason for him to repent, that is, to acknowledge his sin and change his ways.

Unfortunately, Scott's story of coming out to his parents and pastor is far from unique or unusual. Here is another true story, with changed names, that took place in a Christian home.

Tom and Deb were excited. Both of their sons would be home for Thanksgiving. Mark, a senior, was bringing home his girlfriend, Amanda. They had been dating steadily for several months, and Deb felt there might be an engagement announced over the holiday weekend.

Jason, their college sophomore, was also bringing home a friend: his roommate, Zach. Tom and Deb both liked Zach. He was polite, smart, funny, and a big help around the house whenever he visited.

Sure enough, just after the turkey and before the pumpkin pie, Mark announced that he and Amanda would marry soon after his graduation. Tom and Deb were delighted!

Then, right after the pumpkin pie and before the Lions game, Jason announced that he and Zach were lovers, had committed their lives to each other, and hoped that Jason's family would be as happy for them as they were for Mark and Amanda. Tom and Deb were devastated!

Think about it for a moment. What would you do if you were Scott's parents? What would you do if you were Jason's parents, Tom and Deb? What would you do if you were Mark and Amanda? What would you do if you were a friend that either Scott's or Jason's family confided in? What advice would you give?

Certainly there would be prayer—and lots of it. Advice would be sought from trusted Christian friends. There would be law, a reminder that Scott and Jason were sinning against God. There would be encouragement to continue to love Scott and Jason without condoning the sin of practicing homosexuality. There would be encouragement not to drive Scott or Jason away but to share God's Word with them and insist that with God's help, change is possible and necessary. Above all, God's Word would be searched and studied to find the answers and the strength to act in accordance with sound doctrine.

Perhaps one of the most difficult things about homosexuality for a heterosexual is trying to understand it. What causes these sinful, unnatural desires? What causes homosexuality? We turn to God's Word for the answers.

In Proverbs 24:5,6 we read, "A wise man has great power, and a man of knowledge increases strength; for waging war you need guidance, and for victory many advisers." It is good to try to understand the cause of any sin, and specifically the sin of homosexuality, because the more we understand why we are tempted to sin, the more likely we will be to turn to God's Word and find power and strength to overcome it. The homosexual is waging war against deadly desires. A gay person needs guidance and Christian advisers—people who will lend him or her encouragement and support in that personal struggle.

As Scott spoke of his journey, he mentioned that one of the reasons he felt comfortable in his sin of homosexuality was that supposed experts in the medical field were claiming that there was a biological cause for homosexuality. Let's take a brief look at these biological factors.

The most famous study dealing with a possible biological cause of homosexuality was conducted in 1991 by Dr. Simon LeVay, a neuroscientist at the Salk Institute for Biological Studies in La Jolla, California. LeVay studied the brains of 41 human cadavers: 6 purportedly heterosexual women, 16 purportedly heterosexual men, and 19 purportedly homosexual men. His study focused on a group of neurons in the hypothalamus called the INAH3. Supposedly, the INAH3 in the homosexual men was smaller than in the brains of the other cadavers. However, three of the homosexual men actually had a larger INAH3 than the heterosexual subjects. So, 17 percent of his total study group contradicted his own theory. Also, 6 of the purportedly 16 heterosexual men had died of AIDS. LeVay assumed that if a patient's records did not indicate he was homosexual, then he must have been heterosexual. This is a huge shortcoming in the study. Further, in 1992 Dr. Lewis Baxter of UCLA released a study that behavior can produce size changes in the brain. Therefore, even if the INAH3 is smaller in some homosexuals, it may be that the diminished size is caused by the behavior, rather than that the behavior is caused by the size of the INAH3. Finally, LeVay is openly homosexual and after the death of his partner, he said he was determined to find a genetic cause for homosexuality that would affect the legal and religious attitudes towards homosexuality. LeVay and his study were definitely not unbiased!

Homosexuals are still desperately searching for the genetic or biological cause that will allow them to say, "I can't help myself." Homosexuals aren't the only ones to share this goal. Scientists have long been searching for hereditary factors that might predispose a person to alcoholism, for example. And, in fact, it appears that there could be a genetic connection. Someday, scientists may find a hereditary factor that predisposes a person to homosexuality. I don't think they are looking for it, but someday a "gossip gene" may be discovered. But a predisposition does not mean that a person will necessarily become an alcoholic or a homosexual or a gossip. We are all responsible for the ways in which we choose to behave. And if people are intent upon comparing alcoholism and homosexuality, then think about this: As common as alcoholism is, it is not considered to be normal, and millions of dollars and untold hours are spent in its treatment.

But back to the discussion about genes. Today there is a great amount of interest in discovering why so many people are obese. Scientists have discovered that FTO, the "obesity gene," is present in more than half of some populations. A person that received an "obesity gene" from his father and one from his mother is 70 percent more likely to be obese than noncarriers of the gene. But there's good news: your DNA doesn't have to be your destiny. Research shows that you can overcome your genetic predisposition for obesity and be fit and healthy. According to a study by the University of Maryland School of Medicine, exercise can help prevent weight gain even among people who carry the FTO gene.[1]

The important point for us to take from this medical research is that DNA doesn't have to be one's destiny. Genetic predisposition doesn't automatically make you a slave of obesity, alcoholism, gossip, or homosexuality. A person remains responsible for the choices he or she makes in behavior. However, in an age when responsibility is shunned and denied, such a statement is not politically correct, even though it is true.

Supposedly, homosexuals are biologically, constitutionally different from heterosexuals. At the same time, proponents for homosexuality often stress the similarities with heterosexuals in an attempt to dispel homophobia—the fear of or hatred toward homosexuals and homosexuality. Pro-homosexual writers stress the fact that the only difference between homosexuals and heterosexuals is that homosexuals predominantly prefer members of their own sex as objects of sexual desire while heterosexuals predominantly prefer members of the opposite sex for such purposes. Many writers try to further minimize the differences between heterosexuals and homosexuals by classifying all people as more or less bisexual—sexually attracted to members of either sex—stressing that the only difference is sexual preference—a preference for one sex or the other for most of their lives. So while insisting that homosexuals are constitutionally different, pro-homosexual writers also contend that we are all alike. This circular logic is like having your cake and eating it too. And we all know that just isn't possible.

Society thinks that if biology cannot be blamed for homosexuality, then there must be environmental factors that cause it. It is true that there are some things that can be learned about the development of homosexuality. These can help the person struggling with deadly desires and can also be helpful for the person assisting someone in that struggle. Joe Dallas, who has described himself as "a wildly promiscuous kid, a rigidly pious young minister, then a compromised adult who had tried—and failed—to mix Christianity with sexual [homosexual] sin,"[2] offers some thoughts on the development of homosexuality. In coming to grips with his own deadly desires and helping countless others do the same, he has noted a recurring theme in case after case. He believes that homosexual attractions develop along these lines:

1. A child's perception of his or her relationship to parents or significant others.

2. A child's emotional response to those perceptions.

3. Emotional needs arising from these perceptions and responses.

4. The sexualization of those emotional needs.[3]

Dallas concludes that homosexuality fills an emotional need for an individual who has not found a way to fill that need in a normal way. If you find deep satisfaction through homosexual relations and you want that to change, you will need to find the function that homosexuality has served for you. Whatever need homosexuality has fulfilled for you, that need still exists and that need still needs to be met. You will need to fill that need as fully as possible with legitimate and God-pleasing behavior. It can be done; Joe Dallas, and many like him, are living proof of God's power to change and live full lives to his glory.

We need to note that no scientific study on nature or nurture has ever been conclusive in its findings on the cause of homosexuality. Also, all research, to date, is based on speculation with partial information provided by a small group of participants. The conclusions are often drawn by what the researcher wants to find in the data, as well. Even the most celebrated studies are only theory with major flaws in the data. But that should not concern us. The Bible is very conclusive about the cause of sin, including the sin of homosexuality.

In Genesis 6:5,6 we read, "The LORD saw how great man's wickedness on the earth had become, and that every inclination of the thoughts of his heart was only evil all the time. The LORD was grieved that he had made man on the earth, and his heart was filled with pain." The practicing homosexual desperately wants to blame God for his or her sin. Remember Scott's arguments about why he was homosexual? "I never chose to be gay; I was born this way." "From as far back as I can remember, I've always been attracted to guys." "Who would actually choose to be gay? If it were actually a choice, I would've chosen to be heterosexual. My life would be so much easier." "I believe God created certain people to be gay. Why would he do that, if it were a sin?"

Our holy God is not about to take the blame for sin. Sin comes from the thoughts of a person's heart. Sin is man's doing. A person can only blame himself or herself for sin. In a way, the homosexual's argument that he or she was born that way is true. We are all born sinful. But that doesn't excuse our sinful behavior, nor does it nullify our punishment.

Yet the "blame game" continues to be played, and we have become all-star players at it. Much of modern psychology encourages people with problems to blame their parents, childhoods, or anyone but themselves for those problems. Adam was the first to play the blame game. First he blamed Eve, and then even God, for his own sin (Genesis 3:12).

Basketball players used to raise their hand when called for a foul; today they are coached to never acknowledge they committed a foul. Perhaps that isn't such a big deal in a basketball game, but playing the blame game and refusing to take responsibility for our own actions has deadly and eternal consequences in the game of life. If we refuse to accept responsibility for our sin and continually blame someone or something else for our sin, we are lying to ourselves. The apostle John wrote, "If we claim to be without sin, we deceive ourselves and the truth is not in us" (1 John 1:8). If the truth is not in us, then God is not in us (John 17:17). If God is not in us, then the devil is and we belong in hell with him.

Thankfully, the apostle John didn't stop there, though. He went on to write, "If we confess our sins, he is faithful and just and will forgive us our sins and purify us from all unrighteousness" (1 John 1:9). When we take responsibility for our sins and repent of our sins, even the sin of practicing homosexuality, God promises forgiveness and purifies us from our sins. He will give us the strength to overcome our sins, yes, even the sin of practicing homosexuality.

Confession, repentance, and forgiveness result in God's power to change sinful lives. A person who has experienced God's grace and mercy through forgiveness has the power he or she needs to resist temptation. While Scott had "confessed" that he was a homosexual and was practicing that lifestyle, at that point in time he was not repentant. He had no desire to come out of the sin. In fact, he was embracing the sinful lifestyle more and more firmly. Therefore, he was not looking for or experiencing the healing and recovery process. He was rejecting God's forgiveness (because he felt he didn't need it), and he was rejecting God's purification from all unrighteousness. Because our society tolerates, accepts, and embraces the practice of homosexuality, many men and women are in that same situation. They do not know that they are sinning and consequently reject God's forgiveness because they do not know they need it. Today this is a major obstacle in regaining the practicing homosexual for God.

So, the cause of homosexuality is sin. The world plays a role in promoting the sin of practicing homosexuality. However, the person still chooses to follow the wrong path. There may also be biological factors that predispose a person toward the sin of practicing homosexuality, but at this time, there is no reliable scientific evidence for this biological factor. However, even if future, legitimate scientific research discovers a strong genetic factor linked to homosexuality, Christians will continue to follow God's Word and identify the sin of practicing homosexuality for what it is—sin. A genetic predisposition to practicing homosexuality will not excuse the sin or make it "normal" any more than a predisposition to alcoholism excuses that sin or makes it normal. The person is still choosing to follow the wrong path.

In the light of 1 John 1:8,9, we know that those who repent of the sin of practicing homosexuality, and every sin, receive forgiveness through God's Son, Jesus Christ. That forgiveness gives sinners the choice, and the motivation, to turn from that sin.

Rather than repent, however, many people want to excuse their sin. They don't want to acknowledge that homosexuality is a sin that can trap and enslave the perpetrator in much the same way that the abuse of alcohol can lead to the sinful enslavement of alcoholism. When a person reaches the point with homosexuality that an alcoholic does with alcohol, then he or she is a homosexual. This is not a popular view with homosexuals who prefer to rationalize by blaming their sin on someone else, such as parents, society, or even God.

CHAPTER THREE

THE WORD OF GOD—OLD TESTAMENT

SCOTT'S JOURNEY
Part 3: Living Life in the "Land of Oz"
Among a Colorful Cast of Characters

I'm sure almost everyone is familiar with the phrase "stranger than fiction." For over a decade—through the 1990s and early 2000s—the period of time that I was living a life of unrepentant sin as a practicing homosexual, one could probably add that descriptor to some parts of my life.

Many in the gay community I had been exposed to actually contradicted the typical gay stereotypes. They were die-hard sports fans and loved sitting around drinking beer and eating pizza while watching football games. However, some did fit the stereotypes. For example, there were many gay men who truly did have an affinity for show tunes and certain old movies like The Wizard of Oz, The Music Man, Oklahoma, Whatever Happened to Baby Jane, The Sound of Music, *etc. Actresses like Bette Davis, Judy Garland, and Joan Crawford were considered to be royalty by many in the gay community.*

Please note that I'm speaking in generalities here. I am not suggesting that any guy who shows an appreciation for these things should be considered gay.

But what do all of those movies have in common? They're all classic works of cinematic fiction, that is, fantasy. They aren't true, factual accounts of anything that closely resembles reality. There is no real Dorothy, no real place called Oz, much less a real Wizard of Oz.

Hold on to that thought while I introduce you to some people.

Rick *grew up in a rural town in Pennsylvania, a devout member of the Lutheran Church—Missouri Synod. He went on to marry his high school* *sweetheart. After 11 years of marriage, he divorced his wife and came out as a homosexual. For the next 20-plus years, he was in a relationship with another man. He, his male partner, and his ex-wife are all close—the best of friends.*

Dr. Jeff *is an openly gay psychologist. He served as a Roman Catholic priest for over 20 years before he, as he put it, "saw the light," left the ministry, and earned his psychology degree. He hung out his shingle and specializes in the counseling of homosexuals and the families of homosexuals who are* struggling to accept *their sexual orientation.*

Chuck *began his adult life studying to be a Franciscan monk. He left his life as a monk to pursue a naval career. He was married for many years and fathered two children. Later, he left his wife and family after deciding that he was really a homosexual. He ended up with joint custody of his children. He often has his boyfriend sleeping over with him when it is his week or weekend to have his kids. His ex-wife is fine with this.*

Jason *is a closeted gay serving as a high-ranking officer in a branch of the United States military. Jason is someone who definitely benefited from the military's "don't ask, don't tell" policy. However, at one point he found himself in the difficult position of having to sign-off on and support charges against a gay enlisted person in his command who had not been so discreet in his sexual conduct. If Jason hadn't done this, he would have risked drawing attention to himself.*

Pastor Bill *is an openly gay minister of a large metropolitan Christian church. A majority of the congregation is also gay. He routinely dates members of his own congregation.*

As you were reading the brief bios were you perhaps thinking to yourselves, "There's no way those are real people!"? You may be surprised that there's nothing fictional about any of those people (except that their names have been changed). Not only are they real people but they all consider themselves to be practicing Christians. In fact, they were all actual friends of mine over my years of living as an unrepentant homosexual. I still hear from some of them to this day.

Here's where the fiction begins to come into play. For the rest of this section of my journey and into the next section, I'm going to share some of the fiction—the fantasy tales—that is, the ways God's Word has been twisted and perverted by some of those people and many others in the gay "Christian" community.

The title of this chapter points to what Pastor Starr will be talking about next: Old Testament references to homosexuality, that is, what God has to say about the subject of homosexuality in the Old Testament. Pastor Starr asked me to write a little bit about what I experienced in this area. I want to share with you how the Old Testament was being interpreted during my time in the gay community.

"God did speak out against homosexuality in the Old Testament of the Bible." Shocked? Where is the fiction or spin in that statement? I know I was shocked the first time I heard that statement from a practicing homosexual. Some practicing gay Christians actually acknowledge that the Bible and God did speak against homosexuality in the Old Testament. But—and here's the catch (surely, you knew it was coming)—with their next breath they quickly add that the entire Old Testament became obsolete and meaningless *once Jesus Christ died on the cross for our sins. According to them, the New Testament is now the only relevant part of the Bible for the modern-day Christian. The Old Testament is just basically a nice collection of old stories that really don't mean anything to the modern-day Christian. To support this claim, they will make statements like these:*

- *Obviously the modern-day church doesn't still believe in stoning people to death for certain sins.*

- *We're not encouraged to carry out the old eye-for-an-eye directive.*

- *We aren't required to paint blood over our doors for Passover.*

And the list goes on and on.

The gay church that I sometimes attended even advertised itself as strictly a "New Testament church." It treated the entire Old Testament of the Bible as something along the lines of Aesop's fables. That was a pretty effective way to dismiss what God says about the sin of homosexuality in the Old Testament.

26

THE WORD OF GOD—OLD TESTAMENT

As you read that section of Scott's journey, did you come to appreciate the great difficulty for a Christian who is struggling against the sin of homosexuality to overcome that temptation today? Friends who had been married, as well as military personnel, counselors, and ministers were all telling Scott that the practice of homosexuality was good and permissible, even though he had been taught the truth earlier in his life. Churches that call themselves Christian are no longer sounding a clear trumpet call against the sin of homosexuality because it is easier to allow the sin than to fight against it. These churches do a tremendous amount of damage to the souls they try to shepherd.

Let me share an example from my own ministry. It also is a true story, with just the names changed.

Brad and Carol sat in my office, desperate for some help. They had three children under age 9 and didn't know what to do. Carol's dad wanted to visit. The problem was, he had recently divorced Carol's mom and moved in with his male lover. He was also a Lutheran pastor, whose congregation supported him in his decision.

Brad didn't want to have anything to do with him and definitely didn't want him around his children. Carol also condemned her father's actions but still wanted to reach out to him. She still wanted him in her life and the lives of her children.

Amid tears and anger, fear and frustration, we eventually worked out a plan that was acceptable to both Brad and Carol. It was decided that Carol's dad could come for a visit if he came without his gay lover and agreed ahead of time not to discuss his homosexual lifestyle with his grandchildren. It was imperative that he agree to those boundaries before his visit to their home. If he refused to honor their boundaries, he would not be allowed to visit. Carol's father chose his gay lover over his daughter and grandchildren and did not agree to the boundaries. Consequently, he was not allowed to visit.

Carol still held out hope that her father would give up his homosexual lifestyle. Humanly speaking, it is not likely that he

27

will change his sinful lifestyle choice because his church accepts him as a practicing homosexual. He sees his daughter's refusal to accept him as a practicing homosexual to be cold, unloving, and a result of her church's misguided stand on homosexuality. He has assured her that he has forgiven her for her sins against him. Read Genesis 19:4-9:

> Before they had gone to bed, all the men from every part of the city of Sodom—both young and old—surrounded the house. They called to Lot, "Where are the men who came to you tonight? Bring them out to us so that we can have sex with them." Lot went outside to meet them and shut the door behind him and said, "No, my friends. Don't do this wicked thing. Look, I have two daughters who have never slept with a man. Let me bring them out to you, and you can do what you like with them. But don't do anything to these men, for they have come under the protection of my roof." "Get out of our way," they replied. And they said, "This fellow came here as an alien, and now he wants to play the judge! We'll treat you worse than them." They kept bringing pressure on Lot and moved forward to break down the door.

This is a portion of the familiar account of Sodom and Gomorrah. Dr. Martin Luther confessed that he had difficulty simply reading this chapter (*es geht mir durch mein ganzes Herz*—it goes through my entire heart). It is obvious from the words "Where are the men who came to you tonight? Bring them out to us so that we can have sex with them," that the sin of Sodom and Gomorrah was the sin of homosexuality. We see that this sin was so widespread that it affected "all the men from every part of the city of Sodom—both young and old." Homosexuality was tolerated and accepted in Sodom. They had been given over to these shameful lusts and no longer felt any remorse for their sinful behavior. They were not closeted and did not try to hide their intentions, desires, and actions. So blatant was their homosexuality that they shouted their sexual desires aloud, clamoring in the streets of the city. We see similar activity today in the gay pride parades held throughout our country and the world.

Practicing homosexual "Christians" who do not out-and-out reject the Old Testament generally try to spin these clear words of Scripture in one of three ways in order to get them to mean something other than their obvious meaning. They desperately try to make the sin of Sodom and Gomorrah anything but the practice of homosexuality.

1. Professor John Boswell, the author of *Christianity, Social Tolerance and Homosexuality*—the new gay "bible"—states that the real sin of Sodom was inhospitality. He claims that the men of Sodom only wanted to "get to know" the two male strangers who were visiting Lot. Of course, anyone reading the biblical account with an open mind will understand that this is ludicrous. If all the men of Sodom wanted to do was to make the acquaintance of the strangers who were visiting Lot, why did Lot himself urge them, "Don't do this wicked thing"? There is also the matter of Lot offering his own virgin daughters to the men of Sodom for their pleasure. If the men of Sodom had innocent intentions, that offer would have made no sense at all.

2. There are those, including author Virginia Mollenkott, who assert that the sin of Sodom was not homosexuality but attempted rape. "Violence—forcing sexual activity upon another—is the real point of this story."[4] This argument is partially true—the men of Sodom were proposing homosexual rape. But that is only part of the story. Since "all the men from every part of the city of Sodom—both young and old—surrounded the house," homosexuality must have been predominant in the city.

Mollenkott's argument is also weakened by the fact that early literature connects Sodom with general homosexual practices: "The second-century B.C. Testament of the Twelve Patriarchs labels the Sodomites 'sexually promiscuous' (Testament of Benjamin 9:1) and refers to 'Sodom, which departed from the order of nature' (Testament of Nephtali 3:4). From the same time period, Jubilees specifies that the Sodomites were 'polluting themselves and fornicating in their flesh' (16:5, compare 20:5-6). Both Philo and Josephus plainly name same-sex relations as the characteristic view of Sodom."[5]

Read Ezekiel 16:49,50: "Now this was the sin of your sister Sodom: She and her daughters were arrogant, overfed and unconcerned; they did not help the poor and needy. They were haughty and did detestable things before me. Therefore I did away with them as you have seen."

3. Pro-gay authors say that this passage names the sin of Sodom. Again, this argument is partially true. The Sodomites were guilty of sins other than homosexuality: arrogance, gluttony, apathy, unconcern, pride, etc. But as we have plainly seen from Genesis chapter 19, the "detestable things" the Sodomites did before God included—first and foremost—the sin of homosexuality.

Read Leviticus 18:22; 20:13: "Do not lie with a man as one lies with a woman; that is detestable. If a man lies with a man as one lies with a woman, both of them have done what is detestable. They must be put to death; their blood will be on their own heads."

God calls the sin of practicing homosexuality "detestable" (Hebrew: "an abomination"). The divinely prescribed punishment for practicing homosexuality was death. Homosexuality was a capital offense under the theocracy of Israel.

Again, those practicing homosexual "Christians" who do not throw out the Old Testament completely but rather choose to distort its truth have twisted and spun these clear passages to suit their own agendas. Pro-gay authors like Boswell and others (Metropolitan Community Church) assert that these chapters of Leviticus are talking about idolatry, not homosexuality. They claim that Leviticus only forbids the practice of homosexuality in connection with idol worship. After a brief scan of Leviticus 20:7-24, it is easy to refute this pro-gay argument. It should be noted that these chapters of Leviticus also prohibit other sexual sins, such as adultery and incest. All of these sins are forbidden by God in both the Old and New Testaments and not only in the Levitical codes. If homosexuality is forbidden only in connection with idolatry, then all the other practices listed in this chapter (adultery, bestiality, child sacrifice, incest, etc.) are also condemned only in connection with idolatry. Apart from idol worship, they would be acceptable. Of course, such a premise is ludicrous.

However, we must also note that the pro-gay authors do have a valid point. All sin, including the sin of practicing homosexuality, has its root in idolatry. All sin, not just practicing homosexuality, is rebellion against God and puts human will above the will of God. At its base, this is idolatry. God is very clear about this in Romans chapter 1. We'll take a closer look at this in the next chapter.

Judges 19:22-24 is similar to the account of Sodom and Gomorrah, with men of the city, this time Gibeah in Benjamin, clamoring to have sex with a male visitor to the city:

> While they were enjoying themselves, some of the wicked men of the city surrounded the house. Pounding on the door, they shouted to the old man who owned the house, "Bring out the man who came to your house so we can have sex with him." The owner of the house went outside and said to them, "No, my friends, don't be so vile. Since this man is my guest, don't do this disgraceful thing. Look, here is my virgin daughter, and his concubine. I will bring them out to you now, and you can use them and do to them whatever you wish. But to this man, don't do such a disgraceful thing."

Now read Judges 20:46–21:3:

> On that day twenty-five thousand Benjamite swordsmen fell, all of them valiant fighters. But six hundred men turned and fled into the desert to the rock of Rimmon, where they stayed four months. The men of Israel went back to Benjamin and put all the towns to the sword, including the animals and everything else they found. All the towns they came across they set on fire.
>
> The men of Israel had taken an oath at Mizpah: "Not one of us will give his daughter in marriage to a Benjamite."
>
> The people went to Bethel, where they sat before God until evening, raising their voices and weeping bitterly. "O LORD, the God of Israel," they cried, "why has this happened to Israel? Why should one tribe be missing from Israel today?"

Just as he had with the cities of Sodom and Gomorrah, the Lord viewed the behavior of the men of Gibeah as detestable and condemned it and the people who committed and permitted it. The city (and the tribe of Benjamin) was destroyed, not by a miracle of fire and brimstone from heaven but by natural means through war with the Israelites. However, it was difficult for the Israelites to carry out this divine judgment against their brothers.

Similar to their explanation about Sodom and Gomorrah, the pro-gay writers insist that the sin here was *forced sexual activity*, or rape, and not homosexuality itself. The same refutation from God's Word applies.

In the Old Testament, we do often see homosexuality connected with idolatry. This is understandable because in order to practice homosexuality, a person must reject God's clear and undeniable law, which prohibits its practice. Therefore, to be at peace with oneself, a practicing homosexual cannot really worship the true God. The so-called practicing homosexual "Christians" must destroy and deny what God has revealed about himself and his will in the Bible. They claim to worship God, but what they worship is a god of their own creation: a worthless, powerless god that cannot save them. This is so deadly because their false teaching attracts so many weak Christians who are struggling against the sin of practicing homosexuality and convinces them that they can cease their struggle and still be saved. This teaching damns.

The natural knowledge of God teaches people to worship him, but their sinful nature wants to do so only on their own sinful terms. So often, people who want to give their lives over to sin, including the sin of practicing homosexuality, seek loopholes in God's Word. People want to worship God to be on the safe side and yet want to live their sinful lives the way they want to. They do not want to be accountable to God, so they are always looking for disclaimers to his law. They think they find those loopholes in the "gay spin" of what are very clear Bible passages. But God's law is rock solid; it is perfect, having been given by the perfect God, and there are no loopholes.

In spite of that truth, because of the false teaching by some churches regarding homosexuality and because their own sinful natures want it to be true so badly, today many people believe that they can be both practicing Christians and practicing homosexuals. They have accepted homosexuality and identify with the homosexual community. They believe the gay spin on God's clear law. However, they cannot escape the truth of Romans 6:23: "The wages of sin is death." They will ultimately face eternal death in hell for their failure to repent of their sin. The problem is that today homosexuals are being told—by the media, society, and the church—that they are not sinning. Therefore they see no reason to repent.

However, there is also hope in Romans 6:23: "But the gift of God is eternal life in Christ Jesus our Lord." From 1 John 1:9, we know that there is forgiveness when sinners confess their sins. In Ephesians 2:8,9, we read how that forgiveness comes to us, how it becomes our own: "It is by grace you have been saved, through faith—and this not from yourselves, it is the gift of God—not by works, so that no one can boast." Every sinner, including the homosexual, is saved only by grace through faith. This grace and faith are not the work of the individual but of God. They are his gift to us. The repentant homosexual, the repentant adulterer, the repentant thief, the repentant liar, the repentant gossip all receive the forgiveness of their sins in exactly the same way. It is the gift of God through faith in Jesus Christ, and even that faith is the work of the Holy Spirit, not us. When we remember this and believe it, we will not have feelings of superiority over any fellow sinner.

CHAPTER FOUR

THE WORD OF GOD—NEW TESTAMENT

SCOTT'S JOURNEY
Part 4: The Gospel According to the Gay Community

In preparing to write this section of my journey, I sat down, reminisced, and tried to list some Bible passages from the New Testament that would summarize the gay "Christian" community's position on the New Testament. Here is what I came up with:

> *God so loved the world that he gave his one and only Son, that whoever believes in him shall not perish but have eternal life. (John 3:16)*

> *My Father's will is that everyone who looks to the Son and believes in him shall have eternal life, and I will raise him up at the last day. (John 6:40)*

> *[The expert in the law] answered: "'Love the Lord your God with all your heart and with all your soul and with all your strength, and with all your mind'; and, 'Love your neighbor as yourself.'" "You have answered correctly" Jesus replied. "Do this and you will live." (Luke 10:27,28)*

> *Peace I leave with you; my peace I give you. I do not give to you as the world gives. Do not let your hearts be troubled and do not be afraid. (John 14:27)*

Love. Joy. Peace. Happiness. Those four terms pretty much describe the above passages, don't you think? And what's wrong with that? Those Bible verses are all well-known, beloved teachings from Jesus Christ himself, right out of the New Testament of the Bible. They serve as an immense source of comfort for all *believers.*

It's not so much that there's anything wrong with what's there, but with what's not *there! It becomes problematic when those passages are used out of context and apart from the rest of God's Word. To help illustrate my point, I'd like to share the following encounter I had a number of years back.*

One evening I was parking my car in the Dupont Circle area of Washington, DC. That is the hub of Washington's gay community. I was there to meet a group of friends for dinner. As I was parking, a Jeep Cherokee was parking in another space directly in front of me. I couldn't help but notice that the back of this Jeep was adorned with a number of bumper stickers. One was the rainbow flag sticker, which identified this person as openly gay, alongside a sticker supporting a local candidate for political office. Another sticker said, "Live and Let Live," and yet another sticker proclaimed, "Just Do It." But among all of those stickers was one that really peaked my curiosity. It simply said, "John 3:16." The guy who was parking that vehicle proceeded to exit his vehicle just as I was exiting mine. I recognized him as someone I had seen from time to time around that area. Later that evening, after dinner, my friends and I went over to one of the neighborhood bars to continue socializing. There I happened to bump into the driver of that Jeep. We struck up a conversation with each other.

I said to him, "I couldn't help but notice that on the back of your truck you have a sticker that says 'John 3:16.' Are you a Christian?"

This was his response: "Well, I believe in God and all. I went to Sunday school once in awhile as a kid, but I'm not really into all that church stuff now." He went on to say, "I always liked that verse, because I think it pretty much sums up all you need to know about God. And while I don't get into the whole church thing, I have confidence in the fact that knowing Jesus died on the cross is enough to get me into heaven one day."

In a nutshell, that seemed very typical of the attitude most people who were living an unrepentant homosexual lifestyle had toward God and the Bible—at least among those who acknowledged there even is a God. Even in the gay church I attended from time to time, there was never any shortage of preaching or proclaiming the gospel. In hindsight, the problem was with what was rarely preached or discussed—anything related to God's laws. It seems that the attitude of most people who consider themselves to be Christians and yet pursue an active gay lifestyle is that the gospel is basically God's "blank check" given to everyone. As long as you believe in God and Jesus, you are destined for heaven and eternal life.

Fairly recently I wrote an article for my church body's monthly publication. The article was basically a condensed version of the journey I'm sharing in this book. After it was published, I forwarded copies of it to some of my gay friends. I'd like to share with you portions of a response I got back from one guy in particular:

> I was brought up a Roman catholic. You know that the founder of the Lutheran church is Martin Luther (a one-time Augustinian Catholic monk and priest) and that the two Christian denominations are very similar. I was always taught that any sex outside of marriage—straight or gay—is wrong. Sex, according to Catholic (and Lutheran) doctrine is reserved for a man and a wife in marriage for the purpose of propagating the earth. Our churches teach that being gay is not sinful but that practicing gay sex is. I was a seminarian studying to be a Catholic priest for five years. I constantly fought my homosexual desires. I am now 70 years old. I have concluded that God, in His mercy and His love, will look on me and other members of the GLBT (Gay, Lesbian, Bisexual, Transgender) community and, along with other sinners, He will grant us forgiveness. Jesus said to love thy neighbor as thyself. He also taught that among faith, hope, and charity, charity (love) was the greatest. God is love; God is mercy. We don't know why he made people gay or straight but we know that He loves us all. Certainly God does not condemn the love two people of the same sex have for one another.

In response to that, I basically (without much additional commentary) shared the text of 1 Corinthians 6:9-11: "Do you not know that the wicked will not inherit the kingdom of God? Do not be deceived: Neither the sexually immoral nor idolaters nor adulterers nor male prostitutes nor homosexual offenders nor thieves nor the greedy nor drunkards nor slanderers nor swindlers will inherit the kingdom of God. And that is what some of you were."

And to that I received the following additional response:

Scott, I have no desire to argue religion with you. It looks like we'll only agree to disagree. What you are telling me in your emails, I am already well aware of. My beliefs include not only the Bible but tradition as well. At any rate, I'd like you to be a friend. I'd like to see you from time to time but I do not want to discuss your interpretation of the Bible or mine. The fact that we both believe in Christ as our Savior is good enough.

Other portions of the New Testament that many in the gay Christian community hide behind are summarized in the following two New Testament passages.

Do not judge, or you too will be judged. For in the same way you judge others, you will be judged, and with the measure you use, it will be measured to you. (Matthew 7:1,2)

Woe to you, teachers of the law and Pharisees, you hypocrites! You are like whitewashed tombs, which look beautiful on the outside but on the inside are full of dead men's bones and everything unclean. In the same way, on the outside you appear to people as righteous but on the inside you are full of hypocrisy and wickedness. (Matthew 23:27,28)

Wouldn't this issue of the sin of homosexuality be so much easier to address without having to address the larger issue of what sin is in general? I know in Pastor Starr's Bible study, Deadly Desires, and in his comments later in this chapter, he addresses how the gay community spins certain passages of the New Testament that speak specifically against the sin of homosexuality. These friends of mine and others in the gay community would say (and to be honest, in the past I would have joined them), "If you want to break out God's law, then we'll give you a dose of it right back at you. While you may be a heterosexual, the little white lies you tell constantly are no more or less a sin than our choosing to have sexual relations with someone of the same sex. How's that for tit for tat?" In other words, "Everyone is sinful, including you, so leave us alone."

In my experience, many in the gay community are quick to point out that 99 percent of organized churches, and especially conservative churches, are guilty of not following those sections of God's Word.

They quickly point to just about every church scandal in recent times, from the pedophilia scandal involving some priests in the Roman Catholic Church to some of the scandal-ridden televangelists. To them, when you point out or label actions of anyone else as sin, then you are being judgmental and you are sinning. Their general attitude goes back to the slogan on one of the bumper stickers I mentioned earlier: Live and Let Live. I feel that my friend summed up the Christian gay community's attitude quite well in the latter portion of his response to me. Basically, you believe what you want to, and I'll believe what I want. "The fact we both believe in Christ as our Savior is good enough."

THE WORD OF GOD—NEW TESTAMENT

As you can see from Scott's encounter with the gospel according to the gay community, it is quite easy for an uninformed Christian dealing with homosexual temptations to fall prey to the gay community's twisted and not-all-the-truth version of the gospel of Jesus Christ. It is also easy for uninformed Christians who are not tempted by homosexuality to fall prey to the gay spin on the Scriptures. After all, the pro-gay Christian can quote Jesus in the Bible to back up his position. The uninformed Christian may know several gay people in the workplace who are good, hardworking, decent people. Surely God must love them and accept them just as they are—just as we all are being encouraged to do in order to be politically correct. Plus, the laws of our country now make it seem like a hate crime to discriminate or speak against homosexuality, so maybe it is best to just "Live and Let Live."

Of course, that kind of thinking is wrong on so many counts. First and foremost, God does not accept heterosexuals or homosexuals "just as they are." Regardless of sexual orientation, every one of us is a damned sinner by nature. Just as we are, every one of us deserves nothing but eternal damnation in hell. God himself provided the remedy and rescue from our sin and damnation by sending his own Son, Jesus Christ, to be our one and only Savior from sin. However, having our sins forgiven doesn't give us a license to sin. As Paul wrote to the Romans:

What shall we say, then? Shall we go on sinning so that grace may increase? By no means! We died to sin; how can we live in it any longer? Or don't you know that all of us who were baptized into Christ Jesus were baptized into his death? We were therefore buried with him through baptism into death in order that, just as Christ was raised from the dead through the glory of the Father, we too may live a new life. (Romans 6:1-4)

Do Christians continue to sin? Yes, as long as we are on this earth, we Christians sin. Every day we Christians recognize our sins, regret sinning against our holy God, repent of our sins, rely on Christ's full and free forgiveness to cover over all those sins, and resolve to fight against those sins.

The problem in the "Christian" gay community is that the practice of homosexuality usually is not recognized as a sin. There is no regret, no repentance, and no resolve to fight against the sin of practicing homosexuality. Therefore, there is no forgiveness for that sin.

If the practice of homosexuality is recognized as a sin by someone in the "Christian" gay community, it is simply accepted as "that's the way life is." They proudly proclaim, "Everyone sins, but God forgives everyone who believes in Jesus as his or her Savior. I believe in Jesus as my Savior, so my sins are forgiven and I don't have to change a thing." They conveniently ignore the fact that we Christians are to "live a new life" (Romans 6:4), that we are to resolve to fight against sin, even our pet sins. So they may recognize sin, but they do not regret sin, do not resolve to fight against it, and are pushing away the forgiveness Jesus earned for them.

That was exactly the problem with what Scott's friend was saying. "We can sin as much as we want and God will forgive us," he seemed to be telling Scott. When that comes from a 70-year-old man who studied five years for the Roman Catholic priesthood and who still claims to be a Christian while practicing the sin of homosexuality, it has a tremendous impact on a young man who wants to remain a Christian while also wanting to practice the sin of homosexuality.

Of course, the sinful world and our tolerant society love this kind of thinking about sin. Deny sin, or convince sinners that it doesn't matter if they sin. There is an all-out, bare-knuckled attack by American and European society on the truth of Christianity today. As proof of this, we need look no further than the appliance we allow to bring so much filth and anti-Christian propaganda into our homes—the television.

The following is a true story, with the names changed: The kitchen was cleaned up, the children's homework was finished, and finally Sharon could sit down and watch her favorite TV show, *ER*. Her teenage daughter, Rachel, was watching with her. One of the show's story lines revolved around a female doctor's struggle with lesbianism, a struggle she was losing.

Sharon mentioned how disgusted she was with that part of the show and changed the channel. Rachel quickly objected. She said she knew several lesbians at her high school and could understand the attraction. "Boys are so rude, selfish, and clueless about how to make a girl feel good."

Of course, at that point the proper thing for Sharon to do was to turn off the television and have a calm, loving but serious talk with Rachel. She needed to find out what Rachel was really feeling on this subject. Sharon should have known God's Word well enough that she could comfortably turn to it to help correct any misconceptions Rachel may have had on the subject. Sharon and Rachel could have prayed together for those caught in this sin, for our society that is tolerant and accepting of this sin, for the strength to overcome any temptations to this sin, and for the courage and compassion to help others caught in it.

Top-rated TV shows today consistently have a plot, a sub plot, or episodes that show homosexuality in a good or sympathetic light. Even shows on the Home and Garden Television Network promote the homosexual agenda when they show gay and lesbian couples searching for homes on *House Hunters* and portray their living arrangements as normal and natural. Television commercials are also beginning to feature gay and lesbian characters, a reality which proves that sellers are no longer concerned about offending potential heterosexual buyers. The pro-homosexual agenda—deny sin, or convince sinners that it doesn't matter if they sin—finds willing supporters in the media, among politicians, in a tolerant and lazy society, and among misguided Christians.

Let's examine what the New Testament says about the sin of practicing homosexuality as well as how the gay community spins those passages out of context, changes them, or simply denies them in order to continue practicing homosexuality and still feel somewhat religious.

In discussing the sin of practicing homosexuality with a member of the "Christian" gay community, one of the first statements that a person will make is this: "What did Jesus have to say about homosexuality? That's right: NOTHING!" Pro-gay writers insist that since Jesus had nothing to say about homosexuality, he must not have disapproved of it. They reason that if he didn't disapprove of it, then he must have accepted it; he didn't mention it because it was natural among human beings. Some even go so far as to strongly suggest that Jesus and John, "the disciple whom Jesus loved" (John 13:23), had a homosexual relationship. They note that Jesus only had special relationships with men, such as Peter, James, and John. However, Jesus also had close female friends in Mary and Martha of Bethany and Mary Magdalene. When people have convinced themselves that their sin is acceptable, what better way to convince others than to suggest that Jesus did not consider the activity a sin at all but even participated in it himself.

But is it accurate to say that Jesus had nothing to say about the sin of practicing homosexuality? Read the words of Jesus in Mark 10:6-9: "At the beginning of creation God 'made them male and female.' 'For this reason a man will leave his father and mother and be united to his wife, and the two will become one flesh.' So they are no longer two, but one. Therefore what God has joined together, let man not separate." In speaking of human sexuality, Jesus went right back to the beginning of creation (Genesis 2:24) and outlined God's divine plan for human sexuality: male and female, man (husband) and wife. According to Jesus himself, heterosexuality is God's norm.

41

The gay community insists that Jesus was indifferent to sexuality of all kinds, that he did not condemn the practice of sexual intercourse among the unmarried and that he never even remotely spoke of homosexuality. The gay community says that as far as sexuality was concerned, Jesus was only interested in faithfulness. However, Jesus spoke the words of Matthew 15:19: "Out of the heart come evil thoughts, murder, adultery, sexual immorality, theft, false testimony, slander." Certainly, adultery and sexual immorality are not limiting; they refer to sinful sexual activity of any kind among the married and unmarried. But even though Jesus did not specifically address the sin of homosexuality, his apostles and disciples—taught by Jesus and inspired by the Holy Spirit—surely did so in no uncertain terms.

Chapter 1 of Romans is a description of the godless world— strikingly applicable at all times and especially, it seems, at the zenith of so-called intellectual enlightenment. It is a description of what happens when people deliberately transfer the honor due to God, the Creator, to man, the creature. Read Romans 1:25-27:

> They exchanged the truth of God for a lie, and worshiped and served created things rather than the Creator—who is forever praised. Amen. Because of this, God gave them over to shameful lusts. Even their women exchanged natural relations for unnatural ones. In the same way the men also abandoned natural relations with women and were inflamed with lust for one another. Men committed indecent acts with other men, and received in themselves the due penalty for their perversion.

"Because of this" refers to the action of sinful human beings. They worship "created things"—themselves, their own intelligence, money, power, etc.—instead of God, "the Creator." This is unnatural, for certainly the Creator is better than the creation. This fall into unnatural spiritual practices results ("Because of this") in unnatural sexual practices as well—including the practice of homosexuality. The practice of homosexuality is against nature, plain and simple.

Let's take a look at this simple, straightforward, clear passage in the light of the gospel according to the gay community. Basically, the pro-gay authors assert that St. Paul is not condemning homosexuals and homosexuality but only those heterosexuals who engage in homosexual acts. Since homosexuality is not natural for the heterosexual, the heterosexual who practices homosexuality is exchanging "natural relations for unnatural ones." But since homosexuality is *natural* for homosexuals, this portion of God's Word does not apply to them. This can be seen in the argument that author John Boswell offers on these verses:

> The persons Paul condemns are manifestly not homosexual: what he derogates are homosexual acts committed by apparently heterosexual persons. The whole point of Romans 1, in fact, is to stigmatize persons who have rejected their calling, gotten off the true path they were once on.[6]

Paul knew nothing of "sexual orientation" other than the one God created—heterosexuality. In these verses Paul uses the strongest Greek words possible to denote gender and biology. He is definitely talking about men—males—and women—females. What Paul is clearly saying is that it is biologically not natural for a male to have sex with another male and it is not natural for a female to have sex with another female.

In Romans 1:26,27, Paul is talking about people who were given over to shameful lusts and were inflamed with lust for one another. Paul is not talking about people who were forced into a singular homosexual act such as homosexual rape or even those who have experimented with homosexuality out of sinful curiosity and then abandoned it. This is not forced or curious behavior; these people are described as having an intense inner desire for sex with others of their own gender.

Romans 1:26 is the only place in the Bible which speaks directly of female homosexuals. From these verses we can conclude that lesbianism is a violation of nature according to God's order. In fact, the Greek words translated as "exchanged natural relations" depict a frightful exchanging, a horrible trading and perversion. This phrase brings out the enormity of violating even nature itself, established by God. The facts are plain and simple: People—male or female—desiring or engaging in sex with a member or members of their own gender abandon God's given natural order. This is contrary to his holy will. It doesn't matter if they are in a committed, monogamous relationship. It is contrary to God's holy will.

Just as we saw in our study of the Old Testament passages dealing with homosexuality, the pro-gay authors insist that these verses are not condemning homosexuality but idolatry.

> The homosexual practices cited in Romans 1:24-27 were believed to result from idolatry and are associated with some very serious offenses as noted in Romans 1. Taken in this larger context, it should be obvious that such acts are significantly different than loving, responsible lesbian and gay relationships seen today.[7]

Once again, pro-gay authors weave some truth into their argument. However, they fail to see that all sin, including homosexual activity, is the result of idolatry. The practice of homosexuality is a symptom of rejecting a portion of God's Word and God himself.

When men and women take God's honor for themselves, it is an unnatural act in the religious sphere and results in an unnaturalness in the moral sphere as well. Then the natural difference between men and women, placed there by God at creation, is destroyed and both men and women are stripped of their very nature as truly male and female. In an attempt to "modernize" and secularlize God's Word, people refuse to consider God and his revelation worthy of their acceptance. They do not like what they find in God's revelation, and so they ignore or, perhaps even worse, change it to suit their own wishes.

For many in the gay community today, this means denying God's Word while self-righteously claiming they are true Christians. They revel with delight in sin without any pangs of conscience because they have convinced themselves that God is only a God of love. They forget that he is also a just God, a "jealous God," a God who demands that his will be followed by his creatures. Because they forget or ignore God's will, we are told in Romans chapter 1 that God "[gives] them over" to all kinds of sins.

Sexual degradation always follows apostasy—the abandoning of the true faith. Sexual perversion and immorality run wild when man rejects God's control over his life. It was that way in the days of Sodom and Gomorrah, in St. Paul's day, and today.

Look at Main Street America: massage parlors, adult bookstores, adult theaters, gay bars and baths, adult motels where you pay not by the night but by the hour, and pornographic magazines sandwiched between *Time* and *Good Housekeeping*. Most of the "adult" world is open 24 hours a day, seven days a week. The Internet is a 24/7 source of both straight and gay pornography right in our own homes and offices. The lure of just a quick peek at forbidden sexual activity by others has trapped thousands in Internet pornography addiction, costing them jobs, marriages, families, and self-esteem. Yet it is argued that our United States Constitution protects the rights of people to make, distribute, and view such material. As a result, the sun never sets on America's smut. We Christians are supposed to accept all of this as normal and natural.

No matter how loudly and long a person says he believes in God and trusts in Jesus as his Savior, if he willfully rejects God's will and continues to live in sin—like Scott's 70-year-old, one-time Roman Catholic seminarian friend—then he is not really a Christian but an unbeliever.

To help us better understand this point, perhaps it would be good for us to look at the broader context of Romans 1:25-27. Let's look at Romans 1:18-32:

> The wrath of God is being revealed from heaven against all the godlessness and wickedness of men who suppress the truth by their wickedness, since what may be known about God is plain to them, because God has made it plain to them. For since the creation of the world God's invisible qualities—his eternal power and divine nature—have been clearly seen, being understood from what has been made, so that men are without excuse.

45

For although they knew God, they neither glorified him as God nor gave thanks to him, but their thinking became futile and their foolish hearts were darkened. Although they claimed to be wise, they became fools and exchanged the glory of the immortal God for images made to look like mortal man and birds and animals and reptiles.

Therefore God gave them over in the sinful desires of their hearts to sexual impurity for the degrading of their bodies with one another. They exchanged the truth of God for a lie, and worshiped and served created things rather than the Creator—who is forever praised. Amen.

Because of this, God gave them over to shameful lusts. Even their women exchanged natural relations for unnatural ones. In the same way the men also abandoned natural relations with women and were inflamed with lust for one another. Men committed indecent acts with other men, and received in themselves the due penalty for their perversion.

Furthermore, since they did not think it worthwhile to retain the knowledge of God, he gave them over to a depraved mind, to do what ought not to be done. They have become filled with every kind of wickedness, evil, greed and depravity. They are full of envy, murder, strife, deceit and malice. They are gossips, slanderers, God-haters, insolent, arrogant and boastful; they invent ways of doing evil; they disobey their parents; they are senseless, faithless, heartless, ruthless. Although they know God's righteous decree that those who do such things deserve death, they not only continue to do these very things but also approve of those who practice them.

An interesting point on this entire portion of Scripture is that every pro-homosexual writer whom I have read reached the same conclusion concerning this passage. Yet each failed, in varying degrees, to make the proper application. The sins that are listed—lying, idolatry, lust, homosexuality, greed, depravity, murder, etc.—are results, not causes. The cause is explicitly detailed in verse 21: "Although they knew God, they neither glorified him as God nor gave thanks to him."

The cause comes from not worshiping the true and living God. When people no longer love God nor try to live according to his divine will, all sorts of wickedness arise. God turns people over to the sin of practicing homosexuality and all the other sins listed in the chapter. The cause and root of all sin lies in rejecting God as the only true and living God, and in failing to make him our number one priority as the First Commandment demands, "You shall have no other gods before me" (Exodus 20:3). This is evident in the very first sin of Adam and Eve. If we could keep the First Commandment, theoretically we could keep all the others.

The sins of practicing homosexuality, false religion, gossip and boasting—the whole list—are symptoms of the condition of the old Adam within us when we are apart from our Savior Jesus Christ. All of these sins stem from man's basic sin: failure to honor, obey, and worship God as God. Therefore, the person who insists on practicing homosexuality (or any other sin) cannot by definition be a Christian and worship the true God.

Many in the gay community contend that true homosexuality is more than what is described in Romans 1:26,27. They say it is a state of being, a condition that is not chosen by people but is thrust on them by society, physiology, or even God. As believers, we know that because homosexuality is forbidden by Scripture, it cannot come from God. It may come from sinful society; it may even be related to a physiological or psychological disorder in some, perhaps akin to psychosomatic diseases such as some forms of colitis, asthma, migraine headaches, or even certain allergies. But regardless of the cause, the temptation to practice homosexuality may be a person's cross to struggle with through life, just as an alcoholic bears the cross of never being able to take a drink. Like the homosexual, that person must strive, with God's help, to carry that cross without stumbling into sin.

From our study of Romans chapter 1, we see that homosexuality is one part of a bigger picture. It is one aspect of mankind's bondage to sin. Like other sins, the practice of homosexuality is the result of rejecting God and his plan for mankind. As mankind has drawn away from God, God has given mankind over to vile affections and vices.

Part of God's righteous judgment on the sin of idolatry—man not giving God first place in his life—is that God leaves man to his own self-damning devices, leaves him alone, and removes his grace. We dare not fault God for this either, because God grants us his grace; grace is not something we deserve. Grace is God's unmerited favor brought about through Christ's life and death as our substitute. Grace is received through faith. So the practicing, unrepentant homosexual is outside of God's grace, no matter how adamantly he or she insists otherwise. Such a person, like Scott's friend, is in need of God's clear and unchanging law. Then, when recognition and repentance of sin result, he needs God's sweet and comforting gospel, reflected by us, his ambassadors.

Next we turn to two other New Testament passages that clearly condemn the practice of homosexuality.

> Do you not know that the wicked will not inherit the kingdom of God? Do not be deceived: Neither the sexually immoral nor idolaters nor adulterers nor male prostitutes nor homosexual offenders nor thieves nor the greedy nor drunkards nor slanderers nor swindlers will inherit the kingdom of God. And that is what some of you were. But you were washed, you were sanctified, you were justified in the name of the Lord Jesus Christ and by the Spirit of our God. (1 Corinthians 6:9-11)

> We also know that law is made not for the righteous but for lawbreakers and rebels, the ungodly and sinful, the unholy and irreligious; for those who kill their fathers or mothers, for murderers, for adulterers and perverts, for slave traders and liars and perjurers—and for whatever else is contrary to the sound doctrine that conforms to the glorious gospel of the blessed God, which he entrusted to me. (1 Timothy 1:9-11)

We'll consider these two passages together since they are very similar and since the same Greek word is used in both. *Arsenokoi'tai* is translated as "homosexual offenders" and as "perverts." That Greek word was coined by St. Paul, under inspiration, and literally means "males in bed sexually." While the word is unique to Paul, it comes directly from the Septuagint (Greek translation of the Hebrew Old Testament) and the Levitical law code we studied in the previous chapter (Leviticus 18:22 and 20:13). There can be no doubt that Paul is speaking of homosexual behavior.

The pro-gay writers insist that one cannot know to what Paul was referring with his coined word *arsenokoi'tai*. They argue that these verses refer to prostitution or to any man who is immoral, but of course, they cannot refer to homosexuality. However, there is no hint in the word *arsenokoi'tai* of prostitution. The term can only refer to homosexual behavior.

Some comments on the word translated "male prostitutes" in 1 Corinthians 6:9 are also in order. This same word (*malakoi'*) is used in Matthew 11:8 ("What did you go out to see? A man dressed in fine clothes? No, those who wear fine clothes are in kings' palaces") and Luke 7:25 ("What did you go out [into the desert] to see? A man dressed in fine clothes? No, those who wear expensive clothes and indulge in luxury are in palaces"). It means "soft, soft to the touch, delicate." When referring to human beings, it came to mean a man or a boy who allows himself to be used as an instrument of unnatural lust and is effeminate. The authoritative Greek dictionary *Bauer-Arndt-Gingrich* defines it this way: "of persons—soft, effeminate, especially of . . . men and boys who allow themselves to be misused homosexually." This word was often applied to obviously homosexual persons in classical Greek literature.

It appears that this perfectly good Greek word had been distorted in much the same way that *gay,* a perfectly good English word, has come to mean "homosexual" today. The nonbiblical writings of that day do strongly suggest that this word was used to refer to the passive partner—the one who was penetrated—in a homosexual relationship. Today, such a person is usually referred to as a "bottom" as opposed to a "top."

It would appear as though St. Paul in 1 Corinthians 6:9 is naming both the passive (bottom) and active (top) homosexual acts: "male prostitutes . . . homosexual offenders." Both roles are forbidden.

Perhaps a few more remarks about each passage individually are in order. In 1 Corinthians 6:9-11 ("wicked . . . sexually immoral . . . idolaters . . . adulterers . . . male prostitutes . . . homosexual offenders") St. Paul lists sins that were rampant when he came to Corinth. They were gross sins, humanly speaking. The only way to deal with such sinners is to prick their consciences with harsh, stern words of the law: people who live in such sins shall not enter the kingdom of heaven. That word is clear and final. The people to whom St. Paul was writing knew God's law and knew that they had been set free from the bondage of sin by the gospel. But apparently some were in danger of returning to that slavery, feeling that since their sins were forgiven anyway, they didn't need to worry about sin.

So St. Paul writes clearly. In an inspired effort to stem the rising tide of wickedness, he pulls no punches. Paul wanted to make sure that his readers knew, in no uncertain terms, that the liberty given by acceptance of the gospel did not mean libertinism—the right to do whatever they pleased with impunity. God's grace does not give anyone the freedom to sin. So intent was St. Paul to be completely and unequivocally understood that he specifically listed fornicators, idolaters, adulterers, those addicted to sensuality, and homosexuals among those who flagrantly violate the holy will of God. God's people are not to be numbered among those who do such things.

In this passage there is a very important message to homosexual and heterosexual people alike—to all sinners. The message is that *change is possible,* because of our Savior's victory over sin, death, and the devil. That victory is ours by faith. We need to remember to whom St. Paul was writing. He was writing to Christians. And what did Paul say to these Christians? He said that some had been the very sinners he was describing in these verses. Imagine that! Fornicators, idolaters, adulterers, and homosexuals! But they had been changed. By the power of the Holy Spirit working through the means of grace—the gospel in Word and sacraments—they had come to know Jesus Christ as their Savior. They had consequently become new creatures as well, striving to drown their old Adam and sinful lusts every day.

This is true of all Christians for all times. We must remember Christ's promise and its fulfillment and live each day according to our new calling. St. Paul's inspired words are a message of hope to anyone with a propensity toward the sin of homosexuality. He tells us clearly that there is salvation for Christians who have formerly engaged in homosexuality but are no longer continuing in that sinful lifestyle. That's important to remember for other Christians who are not tempted by the sin of practicing homosexuality as well. It is easy to condemn others for a sin that doesn't tempt you, but we are all tempted by sin, we all give in to sin, and there is only one way that we receive forgiveness—by faith in Jesus Christ. In Christ, forgiveness for the sin of practicing homosexuality is as real and valid as is forgiveness for the sins of fornication, idolatry, adultery, gluttony, and gossip.

Unfortunately, the vast majority of psychologists and therapists, as well as many Christian churches, insist that, for the most part, no change in the homosexual is necessary and that indeed change for the homosexual is not possible. This, quite simply, is a lie. Just as with any sin or temptation, for the Christian who must fight against the sin of homosexuality every day, the *possibility of change* is the very heart of the matter. Let there be no mistake about it, change is not easy. As we know from Romans 1:26,27 ("Because of this, God *gave them over*"), homosexuality is a sin that can take over the life of the sinner, just as alcohol can take over the life of the sinner. It is addictive and pervasive. Yet with the help of God, there can be change. There will be more on this in the next chapter.

In 1 Timothy 1:9-11 ("the ungodly . . . the unholy and irreligious; for those who kill their fathers or mothers, for murderers, for adulterers and perverts, for slave traders and liars and perjurers"), St. Paul lists sins, in order, against the Ten Commandments. We note that homosexuality is listed as a sin against the Sixth Commandment—the commandment against adultery. As violators of the Sixth Commandment, St. Paul mentions not only adulterers but sodomites. So he is speaking about people who abuse their fellow men and women for the sake of gratifying their sexual lust in either a "natural" or an "unnatural" way. Both are sinful and both exclude the practitioners from the kingdom of heaven. But this is more than a simple condemnation of illicit sexual acts brought about by force against one party's will. Adultery doesn't have to be rape any more than illicit homosexual acts have to be rape. Adultery between or among consenting adults is wrong just as homosexual acts between or among consenting adults is wrong.

When looking at this passage (1 Timothy 1:9-11), we should draw particular attention to the placement of the words. St. Paul mentions sodomites, or "perverts," immediately after he speaks of "adulterers." He puts them in the same classification. While the reference here is *directly* to *male* homosexuals—sodomites (Genesis 19:5) and abusers of themselves with men (Romans 1:27 and 1 Corinthians 6:9)—within it is an indirect reference to *all* who practice homosexuality, male and female.

As we leave these two passages, it should be obvious that the Holy Scriptures do indeed condemn the sin of practicing homosexuality—homosexuality as it was in St. Paul's day and homosexuality as it is in our own time. Yet it is not a sin from which there is no escape. Thank God, through Christ's redemptive work and sacrifice, there is no such sin! May God's love, that caused him to send his one and only Son to be the Savior of the world, always be reflected by us as we deal with those trapped in the sin of practicing homosexuality. May we recognize that sometimes the strongest and greatest love is firm and hard and tough and always ready to forgive the repentant sinner.

One more reference to homosexuality in the New Testament is found in Jude 7:

> In a similar way, Sodom and Gomorrah and the surrounding towns gave themselves up to sexual immorality and perversion. They serve as an example of those who suffer the punishment of eternal fire.

The Greek words translated "gave themselves up to . . . perversion" literally mean "going away after different or strange flesh." From our study of Romans 1:26,27, we know that this perversion (different or strange flesh) is a reference to exchanging natural relations for unnatural ones. This is obvious also from the reference to Sodom and Gomorrah. Jude is referring to the sin of practicing homosexuality. However, this passage should only be used to condemn the sin of practicing homosexuality when it is used in connection with other clear passages of Scripture referring to this sin.

Of course, the gay community refuses to see this clear and obvious reference to their sin of choice. All the same flimsy arguments used against the clear words of Scripture in Genesis chapter 19 and Romans 1:26,27 are employed here in Jude 7. The same refutation from Scripture also applies. Some pro-gay writers even suggest that Jude is referring to the Jewish legend that the *women* of Sodom had sexual relations with the angels, disguised as men, who visited Lot. One can almost understand how such a legend may have arisen. To the women of a city filled with homosexual men, two apparently heterosexual men must have seemed heaven-sent.

It is obvious that this verse does not refer to the Jewish legend regarding the women of Sodom because of the clause "gave themselves up to sexually immorality and perversion." The wording shows that this was not a onetime occurrence but a lifestyle engaged in by many people in Sodom, Gomorrah, and the vicinity.

In conclusion, the Scriptures are very explicit in their condemnation of the sin of practicing homosexuality. The person who lives in such sin is plainly excluded from the kingdom of heaven, as is the fornicator, idolater, and adulterer. It is also clear from 1 Corinthians 6:11 that "once a homosexual, always a homosexual" is no more a truism than the statement "once a drunk, always a drunk." There may have been a predisposition for the sin from birth. There may have been factors that nurtured the temptation. There may always be a propensity for this particular sin. But, as with any sin, with the help of the Holy Spirit and fellow Christians, people can resist the temptation of practicing homosexuality. Homosexuality, like many sins, is a sin that enslaves, but it is also, like all sins, a sin from which our Savior has freed us.

Unfortunately, homosexuality will continue to enslave and damn any who refuse to acknowledge it as sin or who are duped by those claiming to be theologians and Bible scholars and who say that it is not a sin but a viable alternative lifestyle. Some in the gay community would even have us believe that the people of biblical times were completely unfamiliar with the terms and concepts of homosexuality. They remind us that modern psychologists and sociologists have given us the terms *heterosexual, homosexual, bisexual,* and *sexual orientation.* They would have us believe that the ancient prophets, apostles, and evangelists who wrote the Old and New Testaments by inspiration of the Holy Spirit had no concept of these things.

What they are saying, in effect, is that God's inspired Word is no longer applicable for our enlightened age. They ask us to pity the poor writers of the Bible who could only call a sin a sin instead of some fancy word that was concocted to give validity and respectability to man's basest desires and his rebellion against God's will. In 1913 Gertrude Stein wrote, "A rose is a rose is a rose." The ancients knew what homosexuality was—regardless of the name given it.

At this point, perhaps a brief summary of the Gay Community's contentions regarding the biblical injunctions against the sin of practicing homosexuality is in order. First, most from the gay community agree that the only place the Bible clearly prohibits homosexuality and homosexual relations is in Leviticus. They quickly dismiss this prohibition of homosexuality because it called for the death of those who practiced homosexuality. They insist that the death penalty is not in keeping with the ideals of the Christian community today and so must be dismissed as not applicable in our day and age. Second, the gay community suggests that the account of Sodom and Gomorrah does not condemn the sin of practicing homosexuality but poor manners in regard to hospitality. Third, people in the gay community try very hard to convince us that the New Testament passages speak only of heterosexual persons who engage in homosexual activity. This, they claim, is wrong because it is against the nature of a heterosexual. Since homosexual acts come naturally to homosexual persons, St. Paul and St. Jude were not condemning homosexuals. Finally, the gay community insists that the passages we have studied in this chapter must be considered in the light of modern psychology, sociology, and psychiatry, none of which are exact sciences.

Overall, the gay community insists that we believe that *man's* will must be placed above *God's* will because it is not convenient or contemporary to accept the good and perfect will of the almighty and gracious Creator, Redeemer, and Sanctifier.

The Simon and Garfunkel song "The Boxer" includes the following line: "All lies and jest, still a man hears what he wants to hear and disregards the rest." What a sad but accurate description of people in the pro-gay community and their approach to God's divinely inspired Word! They hear only what they want to hear, and they do not want to hear any condemnation of homosexuality. May none of us fall into the same trap of hearing only what we want to hear when it comes to God's Word.

What a testimony to the power of the Holy Spirit working through the means of grace—the gospel in the Word and sacraments—is Scott's exodus from the gay lifestyle! In spite of the lying spin put on clear Bible passages by the so-called Christian gay community, the Holy Spirit kept working in Scott's heart through his baptismal grace for the decade during which he chose this sinful lifestyle. Even though "Christians" in the gay community were telling Scott his practice of homosexuality was not sinful, that it was natural for him, the Holy Spirit kept whispering to Scott's heart that what he was doing was wrong. Using many different people and events, including a positive HIV diagnosis, the Holy Spirit kept calling to this precious blood-bought soul to return to the Lord. By God's grace and power, Scott has.

CHAPTER FIVE

THE CHANGE

SCOTT'S JOURNEY
Part 5: "Out of the Depths I Cry to You, O Lord"

To recap briefly the previous four sections of my journey, let me remind you that for over a decade I had been living life as an unrepentant homosexual. I had immersed myself in the gay community and especially the gay "Christian" community. As a result, I was more or less comfortable with my decision to live life as a practicing gay Christian. I had surrounded myself with other gay Christians. I felt as if I were now living my life as God meant for me to live it. I erroneously felt God had created me that way: gay. My gay Christian friends reinforced that feeling. I erroneously felt I had been victimized by my ultraconservative Christian upbringing, making me feel guilty for my sexual preference when I felt I should have been celebrating it. Again, my gay Christian friends reinforced that feeling. I had become content, living in the depths of unrepentant sin.

In the eyes of society, I would have been considered a tremendously wonderful and successful human being. As I shared previously, already as a teenager in high school I had become involved in the local volunteer rescue squad and had eventually become an emergency medical technician (EMT). As an adult I had furthered that line of education by becoming a fully certified EMT—paramedic with the National Registry of Emergency Medical Technicians. That is the top level or tier of that professional track. I quickly excelled in my chosen profession. At a fairly young age, I obtained a paramedic position, considered to be the height of prestige in the emergency medical services field. I was hired as a medevac (helicopter) paramedic for one of the oldest and most prestigious medevac programs on the East Coast. It is affiliated with the biggest trauma and burn center in the metropolitan Washington, DC, area. I was respected by my professional peers and was very popular and desired in the gay community. I never felt alone. I had lots of friends. Almost always there were other attractive guys seeking to date me, wanting to become my boyfriend. These were guys who would have made any girl jealous. These were the kind of guys that fit the cliché: All the great guys are either married or gay.

—Although I was living in the depths of unrepentant homosexual sin, in a way I felt as if I were on top of the world in many aspects of my life. Life couldn't get much better.

However, throughout this time in my life I continued to have a nagging sense in my heart and conscience that all was not right with my lifestyle choice. Though if you would have asked me about my lifestyle at that time, I would have been spouting the gay community's party line: This wasn't a choice I had made. I had been born that way, and I was still a child of God.

The Holy Spirit, however, never stopped working in my life. Looking back with 20/20 hindsight, I now feel that because of my stubbornness, God the Holy Spirit had to take some drastic measures to get the point across to me and convince me that, in fact, I was not leading a God-pleasing life.

How did that transpire? Allow me to share the saga. This is a part of my life that some people (there are not many who know all the pieces of this story) have said is stranger than fiction.

I had begun feeling ill at times without any logical explanation. It was not flu season and I didn't have food poisoning, but I was feeling similar symptoms. I had practiced "safe sex" most of the time, but not always. Because of my background in health care, I knew more than most people the risks of unprotected sex. In addition, I had many friends who had died of AIDS and knew the gay community mantra: get tested (for HIV), practice safe sex, get tested. But, for whatever reason, I didn't always.

At that time I accepted an even more prestigious job at the large hospital where I had been working as a medevac paramedic. I had taken a position as the Clinical Assistant to the Director of Interventional Cardiology—the cardiac catheterization laboratory—at the hospital. It *was almost unheard of that someone like me, a paramedic, would attain such a prestigious position. In that position I generally worked 13-14 hour days, five days a week. I rarely got as much sleep as I should have, rarely ate well, rarely got enough exercise, etc. So at first I wasn't all that alarmed by the steady weight loss and increasing fatigue that I was experiencing. Finally, I was pretty much incapacitated for a week by a severe flulike illness, only it wasn't flu season. I reached the point where some of my friends, who were also health-care professionals, contacted my boss and shared with him how sick I was. He arranged for me to be immediately admitted to the hospital where he and I worked. Because of his position, I had some of the best doctors in the region taking care of me. They put me through an exhaustive battery of tests, trying to determine the source for my unexplained viral illnesses and recent general decline in health. They weren't able to pinpoint anything definitive until one of them finally asked the question of all questions: "Scott, when was the last time you had an HIV test?" At the time I evaded the question, defiantly ruling that out as a possibility. So my diagnosis at that time was "Acute Viral Illness of Unexplained Origin," which basically meant that I was very sick and the doctors couldn't figure out why. After a couple days in the hospital, I got better, and after a few more days of resting at home, I went back to work.*

However, that one doctor's question, "When was your last HIV test?" continued to haunt me. HIV? Could it be? Me with HIV? As a healthcare professional myself, I knew that there was little else that could be causing my decline in health. The doctors had pretty much confirmed that by asking the question while I was hospitalized.

Finally I made an appointment with my primary care physician to go in and have an HIV test. Today you can have a mouth swab that will test for the presence of HIV nearly instantly with a high degree of accuracy. But back then the test still required having your blood drawn and sent away to a lab for analysis. A number of days would pass before I could get a return appointment to find out my results. I'll never forget that those few days felt like a year! Time could not have moved along any more slowly. I remember that I was so disturbed about the potential results, I felt the need to stay with some friends. I could not bear to be alone. They even drove me to the doctor's office and sat with me on the fateful day I got my results.

I'm sure most of you can guess what the results were. As my doctor would explain, I did indeed test positive for HIV. Not only that, but by the appearance of some of my other lab results, I had been HIV positive for quite a while. This was not something that I had just come down with.

I was devastated! *I felt it was tantamount to being diagnosed with an aggressive terminal cancer or receiving a death sentence as a verdict from a courtroom jury and judge. I felt like the wheels had suddenly begun flying off of my otherwise rosy life. And yet, I tried to go back to work and resume some sort of normalcy. But that wasn't meant to be.*

My boss, while not a religious man, was extremely conservative. I had often heard him make disparaging slurs and comments about gays. So all the while that I was in his employ, I had carefully kept my personal and professional lives completely segregated. However, I took note that my boss, the Director of Interventional Cardiology, had suddenly become very distant and cool toward me. Shortly after I returned to work, I began receiving random disciplinary notices for really nonsensical things. Before this time I had only ever received his glowing praise for a continual job well done. He had complimented me for always giving 110 percent and for excelling in my position. I was perplexed. After all, I hadn't shared any of what had transpired with anyone at the hospital. However, things quickly began to take an even darker turn. One of my boss' physician partners pulled me aside and warned me that I needed to start watching my back. He informed me that through some less than ethical avenues, my boss had found out what was wrong with me and had stated, "I can't have a sick person like that continuing to work for me." At the same time, my new infectious disease specialist was cautioning that I could not continue the demanding schedule and hours that my job had historically required. So my boss' concerned partner wisely suggested that I take an immediate medical leave of absence and consult with a good lawyer as soon as possible. Another concerned coworker was able to provide proof that my boss and some of his partners had been doing things like reading some of my personal e-mails, illegally accessing some of my private medical and lab records, and doing several other underhanded things. I felt as if I had suddenly become a character in some dark cloak-and-dagger novel. As much as I had felt that my life was falling apart before, it was nothing compared to what I now felt. Basically, it was like being on an airplane whose engine had failed and was spiraling out of control toward the earth!

As you might imagine, I entered into a phase of very severe depression. I was prescribed all sorts of psychiatric drugs to treat the depression, as well as severe anxiety, and began regular sessions with a psychologist. (Remember Dr. Jeff, whom I introduced in chapter 3?) I had enough evidence against my boss that his attorneys made him see the necessity of reaching a quick settlement with me. With the benefit of the disability income and settlement money and because of the profound depression, I stayed out of work for the next year.

During that year, with the help of God the Holy Spirit, I finally began to connect the dots of my life. I was able to see where I had been and how I had chosen to succumb to and live a life of unrepentant sin. At that time the Holy Spirit was working overtime in my life to help me begin to see what always should have been apparent but what I had refused to acknowledge before then. I had been living a life of unrepentant sin, and God was making it brutally clear to me that there were real consequences *of those sins.*

Many people have criticized me for making the above statements. They have reminded me, and I would wholeheartedly agree, that HIV and AIDS are not just "gay diseases." AIDS is not a disease whose single purpose is to enact punishment on those living an unrepentant sinful lifestyle. Some have contracted AIDS and died from the disease as a result of receiving tainted blood transfusions (prior to the days of screening blood donors for HIV). Others have contracted the disease from a spouse who may have gotten it by cheating in their marriage. Of course, I am reminded also of the fact that bad things do indeed also happen to good people.

Having said that, I must go back to what I've said earlier: I believe that in my particular case, my sinful stubbornness and the erroneous belief that I was living a God-pleasing life as a practicing homosexual required more drastic measures to snap me out of the cycle of unrepentant sin and self-destruction with which I seemed to be content. To use Pastor Starr's analogy with alcoholism, I personally needed to hit rock bottom—really hit bottom (which you can see I truly did)—before I would snap out of it.

Even with all that had gone wrong in my life, it wasn't as if I woke up the next day or the next week and suddenly said, "Oh, I get it now. I've been living a life of unrepentant sin and that has to stop." No, absolutely not! But the events in my life were the catalyst that forced me to think. This was only the beginning of my multiyear journey back to God with the help and guidance of the Holy Spirit.

One of the turning points of the journey came the day I happened to pick up and blow the dust off a book my dad had sent me back when I had first come out to my parents. It was a book for Christians trying to overcome homosexuality. Even though over the years I had refused to ever give it serious consideration, that day I picked it up and began reading it. As I read the things the author said and about the struggles with homosexuality that others had endured in their personal journeys, the Holy Spirit opened my heart and mind to actually hear and understand some of the content of that book. Before this I had shrugged off what little I had read as complete and utter nonsense. But here's another thing for which I have to credit the work of the Holy Spirit: While I had scoffed at the book for over a decade, I had never thrown it out. For no reason that is apparent to me, I had held onto it.

After months on antidepressant medications and weekly counseling sessions, I really didn't feel any better. I was looking for answers and for peace of mind. But neither the medications nor the professional counseling were providing those. Then one day I began literally to cry "out of the depths" and to honestly and earnestly pray to God for help. This is what I should have been doing from the beginning. But as it is said, hindsight is always 20/20. I began reading and praying on a more regular basis. The book from my dad contained several prayers. The author encouraged those who were trying to overcome homosexuality to make it a habit of praying those prayers. The next step was to blow the dust off of my Bible and reimmerse myself in the Word of God. Only this time, I immersed myself in the complete Word of God, not just the gospel passages that were ripped out of context and sounded so rosy when smeared with the gay spin I shared at the beginning of chapter 4. I also turned to several of the passages that Pastor Starr will be sharing with you in his portion of this chapter as well as some others.

After a period of regular prayer and study of the Word of God, with the help of the Holy Spirit I took the next step and reached out to some pastors who had greatly influenced me while I was growing up. It took some time and effort on my part to track down one of them, as he had long since moved on from my home congregation. Then, after they coaxed, encouraged, and urged me to return, I finally went back to church—and not the liberal, pro-gay church that I had attended for a time. I went back to a church of the Wisconsin Evangelical Lutheran Synod.

I know this section of my journey has been long and drawn out. But there is one point I personally would like to drive home to everyone who has been reading this. It's the fact that it wasn't my parents, nor any of my relatives, nor any friends from church, nor even the pastors who continually peppered me with God's law, that in the end were successful in guiding me back to my God and Savior. It was the work of God the Holy Spirit, who from my baptism and throughout my entire life has continued to work in me. The Holy Spirit was successful. However, when I say he guided me back, I am giving you a teaser, or preview, of the next section of my journey. I will merely say for now that I never woke up one day and felt I had been miraculously transformed into a heterosexual. You'll have to stay tuned for chapter 6 to hear more about that.

THE CHANGE

Mention a cure for homosexuality to one of its advocates and the reaction can verge on violent. This should not surprise us. It is not all that unusual in other areas of sin. Our own reaction is often similar when we realize that we must not indulge in our own pet sin, whatever that may be.

Our old Adam, that is, our sinful nature, constantly rebels against God's will. It is always looking for ways to excuse and even nurture the sin that continually raises its ugly head in our lives. We have the most difficulty controlling our sinful urges when we are tempted by our pet sins. Therefore, we can expect that someone who is caught in the sin of practicing homosexuality will vehemently defend his or her right to practice that sin. But no matter what defense is offered for this lifestyle, homosexuality remains a sin against God. Because practicing homosexuality is a sin, the Christian, out of love and thankfulness for all that God has done for him or her, will seek to avoid it. The person who has been practicing homosexuality and also wants to live a God-pleasing life must change his or her lifestyle so that it no longer includes the practice of homosexuality. By the grace of God and through the power of the Holy Spirit, change for the homosexual is possible. But that change is often difficult because of the pervasive and consuming nature of the sin. It is made all the more difficult because society and even some Christian churches proclaim that no change is necessary. Or they preach that change is not possible.

Yet people change destructive behaviors all the time. As their friends, we try to help them make that change. For example, what would you do if a friend of yours engaged in behavior that would likely result in the following?

- A significantly decreased likelihood of establishing or preserving a successful marriage

- A five- to ten-year decrease in life expectancy

- Chronic, potentially fatal, liver disease—hepatitis

- Frequently fatal esophageal cancer

- Pneumonia

- Internal bleeding

- Serious mental disabilities, many of which are irreversible

- A much higher than usual incidence of suicide

- A very low likelihood that these adverse effects can be eliminated unless the condition itself is eliminated

- Only a 30 percent likelihood of being eliminated, and then generally only after lengthy, often costly, and very time consuming treatment[8]

You should also know that while genetics may play a role, the condition described above is caused by behavior. Even though the condition is destructive, people choose to continue the behavior. Many people with the condition deny that they have a problem and resist all attempts to help them change. Often people with the condition socialize almost exclusively with others engaging in the behavior. If a loved one or someone you care about was caught in such destructive behavior, what would you do?

Would it help you to know that the condition just described is alcoholism? Wouldn't you do everything you could to help the person eliminate this behavior from his or her life? Wouldn't you do everything you could to help the person make healthy lifestyle choices?

What would you do for a loved one or friend who engaged in behavior that would likely result in these similar problems?

- A significantly decreased likelihood of establishing or pre-serving a successful marriage

- A *25- to 30-year* decrease in life expectancy

- Chronic, potentially fatal, liver disease—infectious hepatitis—which increases the risk of liver cancer

- Inevitably fatal immune disease including associated cancers

- Frequently fatal rectal cancer

- Multiple bowel and other infectious diseases

- A much higher than usual incidence of suicide

- A very low likelihood that these adverse effects can be elim-inated unless the condition itself is eliminated

- An at least 50 percent likelihood of being eliminated through lengthy, often costly, and very time-consuming treatment[9]

You should also know that while genetics may play a role, this condition is caused by behavior. Even though the condition is destructive, people choose to continue the behavior. Many people with the condition deny that they have a problem and resist all attempts to help them change. Often people with the condition socialize almost exclusively with others engaging in the behavior. If a loved one or someone you care deeply about was caught in such destructive behavior, what would you do?

This condition is homosexuality. You can see the striking similarities between the two conditions, both of which have their root cause in the individual's choice of behavior.

You've now read Scott's description of the devastation his diagnosis with HIV and AIDS (Acquired Immune Deficiency Syndrome) has caused in his life. He lost the career he loved and was good at—a nationally registered EMT–paramedic. He now works at testing burglar alarms. He had been very popular, with lots of friends and guys wanting to have a relationship with him. He now has a much lonelier existence. Of necessity he can't continue friendships with actively gay men, and yet, he doesn't completely fit in with his heterosexual friends either. He went from being healthy, energetic, and robust to needing a cocktail of prescription medications to help him function throughout the day. He has lost so much, and yet gained everything!

Both alcoholism and homosexuality incur a tremendous cost for the individual and for society. Yet society and individuals respond much differently to people caught in alcoholism compared to those caught up in an active homosexual lifestyle. While treatment for alcoholism, often defined as a medical disease or a disorder, is readily available and sometimes covered by medical insurance, similar treatment for homosexuality is generally unavailable. Treatment for alcoholism focuses on the individual and the elimination of the destructive behavior. An abundant system of support groups are available. Treatment for homosexuality focuses on making the behavior safer and treating the consequences so that the individual can continue the behavior. Support groups are not readily available.

There are several reasons why traditional support groups for those struggling with the sin of practicing homosexuality do not generally work. Let me illustrate one. The last place you would expect to find an Alcoholics Anonymous (AA) meeting would be in a bar or saloon. The reason is obvious: people struggling with an addiction to alcohol are going to be tempted by the easy availability of alcohol in such a place. A bar may bring back memories of pleasure or escape, of times when life was "easier" without the struggle against the addiction. In the same way, for a man struggling against the sin of practicing homosexuality, sitting in a room with a group of men who are sexually attracted to other men can in itself be a temptation. The same is true for women. Recovering alcoholics come to depend on other people in their meetings for emotional support. Those struggling with the sin of practicing homosexuality also develop emotional ties to other people in their group. The problem is that for the homosexual, those emotional ties can and often do lead to a sexual encounter or relationship.

Another reason for the failure of traditional support groups for those struggling against the sin of practicing homosexuality is that heterosexuals often have an extremely difficult time understanding the attraction of homosexuality because they have never experienced it. For example, it is extremely difficult to find a straight guy who is comfortable befriending a gay guy who wants to come out of the sin of practicing homosexuality or who can effectively mentor that person. The stigma against this sin, the natural fear of something one does not understand, and the revulsion many heterosexuals have for a temptation and sin against which they have never had to struggle keep many good Christian men and women from feeling that they could help someone in his or her struggle against the sin.

Scott has been blessed with a Christian congregation that accepts and supports him in his struggle against the sin of practicing homosexuality. The Holy Spirit has blessed Scott with an amazing courage to come forward with his story in the fervent prayer that it will help others who are also struggling against this particular sin. Scott has had experience with counseling and support groups that did not work or that focused on changing behavior without changing the heart. As he has shared his story with pastors and lay leaders in our church body, others struggling against the sin of practicing homosexuality have reached out to him. In an effort to help others in their struggle against this temptation, Scott has set up an online support group. He is seeing some success with this effort, and we pray that the Holy Spirit will continue to bless it. From time to time Scott calls me with a hard question from the group, and I try to serve as a spiritual advisor, as do several other pastors. If you would like to be a part of that online group, you can contact Scott Barefoot on Facebook.

Support for those struggling against the temptation to practice homosexuality is crucial. We know from God's Word that unrepented homosexual behavior damns; it excludes one from the kingdom of God. We also know that homosexual behavior can be highly destructive to one's health and earthly longevity. The sin of practicing homosexuality is enslaving; it is addictive. For the person seeking release from its powerful grip, it can seem impossible. Sinful society screams that change is not necessary for the homosexual, that change is actually contrary to the homosexual's nature. Yet God tells us in Mark 10:27, "Jesus looked at them and said, 'With man this is impossible, but not with God; all things are possible with God.'" Man, without God, does find change from sinful behavior impossible. That is why society insists that change is not needed or possible. Our Savior Jesus assures us that with God in our lives, such change is possible and necessary.

This is true for every addiction, whether it is to alcohol, legal or illegal drugs, overeating, shopping, or the sin of practicing homosexuality. Addiction is the experience of being unable to immediately and permanently stop the behavior without suffering some degree of discomfort. The very behavior once sought to fill an emotional void and bring pleasure becomes the slave driver. This behavior is seen in the homosexual lifestyle, which often seeks multiple partners and anonymous sex in darkened theaters, baths, restrooms, or from the Internet. This addictive behavior, exhibited in the alcoholic, drug abuser, homosexual, glutton, shopaholic, and others, definitely has its roots in idolatry. The behavior puts its own satisfaction in God's place in our lives. The behavior takes over first place in a person's life. The apostle Paul gives us the only true way to be set free from the enslavement of an addiction in Philippians 4:19: "My God will meet all your needs according to his glorious riches in Christ Jesus." Only through a close relationship with God can the addiction be forced from its place of prominence in one's life and daily drowned. Only God can meet all our needs, including the need that the addiction once filled for us.

The church is in a unique position to offer the help that is needed. Yet it is a sad fact of history that the Christian church has not always been as ready to reflect Christ's love to the homosexual as the Bible instructs. Without treating sin lightly or taking it for granted, we must also extend the helping hand of Christ's love to all who are in need. To be sure, we must use the law to convince the individual of his or her sinfulness. But we must also be ready to assure the repentant person of God's forgiveness. We need to follow the example of our Savior when he dealt with an adulterous woman (John 8:1-11). First he told the woman that he did not condemn her. Then he told her to leave her life of sin. He showed love for her by saving her from execution. Out of love and thankfulness for her salvation through Christ, the adulterous woman was to leave her life of sin. First came Christ's love and salvation (which did not condone her sinful lifestyle), then came Christ's command to change. So often churches and Christians do the opposite. They tell the homosexual or others caught in "public" sins to change and then the church will love them. This is one area where the church often does need to rethink its reaction to the sin of homosexuality. We Christians need to be ready to help anyone fighting the temptations of sin—homosexual or otherwise. If that person is troubled by homosexuality, then we should be eager to encourage the struggle against it, to rejoice at the triumphs over it, and to help pick up the person after a fall into that sin.

Jesus Christ has given us an example to follow. Here we think of our Savior's parable of the prodigal son (Luke 15:11-32). This son offended his father, fell deeply into sin, and almost despaired. When he repented of his sin and returned to his father, he was welcomed with open arms. His father even killed the "fattened calf" in order to celebrate in the best possible way. We think also of Simon Peter, who was lovingly reinstated to discipleship after his sin of denial of our Savior (John 21:15-19). We need to love the person struggling against the sin of practicing homosexuality with Christ's love—a love that never condones sin but is always ready to extend a Christian helping hand in the fight against it. We must never turn away from that person because of fear or revulsion. We must be approachable.

Many churches and Christians are reaching out with the powerful love of Christ. Some go too far and hallow the sin of practicing homosexuality, thus making the fate of the sinner worse than before. In an attempt to be contemporary and politically correct, many churches today choose the easier road of changing God's Word and defending and excusing homosexual actions among Christians instead of undertaking the more difficult task of helping the homosexual to change sinful behavior. Such churches cannot possibly offer the homosexual the help he or she so desperately needs. By ignoring God's judgment against the sin of practicing homosexuality, they also take away Christ's grace, which is necessary to overcome the sin. This is the kind of gay Christian church Scott had found and attended at times. While that church allowed Scott to continue in his sinful lifestyle with the outward pretense of being a Christian, Scott's conscience, instructed by the Holy Spirit, would not let him accept the damnable lie as truth. Praise be to God!

So enslaving is the sin of practicing homosexuality that a permanent "cure" may not be possible. That is, it may never be possible for a homosexual to have a life free from homosexual temptation. But it is not impossible for a homosexual to change. It is not impossible for a homosexual to resist that temptation. Speaking of salvation, our Savior said, "With man this is impossible, but not with God; all things are possible with God" (Mark 10:27). Change does not come easily for sinful human beings. Only through the power of the Holy Spirit, working through the means of grace (the gospel in the Word and the sacraments), can any person change his or her sinful life.

From God's Word it is possible to formulate a five-step program for overcoming addiction and temptations that prove persistent and pernicious.

Step 1: *Reveal* the addicting sin. The psalmist David had personal experience with unrepented sin. After his sins of adultery and murder, King David experienced the guilt of conscience and uneasiness that Scott described during the decade of his entrapment in the sin of practicing homosexuality. While both King David and Scott gave the outward appearance that all was fine in their lives, inside it was a different story, thanks to the work of the Holy Spirit. The psalmist David described that feeling and gave inspired advice to all of us in two of his psalms: "When I was silent and still, not even saying anything good, my anguish increased. My heart grew hot within me, and as I meditated, the fire burned; then I spoke with my tongue" (Psalm 39:2,3). "When I kept silent, my bones wasted away through my groaning all day long" (Psalm 32:3). The sin must be confessed to God, but it also must be confessed to others who are able to hold you accountable to proper behavior in love. The homosexual must find someone to whom he or she can reveal the desire to engage in homosexual behavior and count on that person for help in overcoming that desire and temptation. If your addiction includes the use of the Internet, consider signing up for accountability with a site such as covenanteyes.com, which sends a report of every site you visit on your computer to people you choose to hold you accountable. For example, I currently serve as an accountability partner for Scott.

Step 2: *Release* the sinful behavior that is defiling you. Without a willingness to stop the behavior, the person will miss the grace of God. The writer to the Hebrews expounds on this step in 12:14,15: "Make every effort to live in peace with all men and to be holy; without holiness no one will see the Lord. See to it that no one misses the grace of God and that no bitter root grows up to cause trouble and defile many." The desire to want to stop the addictive and/or sinful behavior must come from an understanding of God and his grace. Only when we understand what our Savior has done for us to save us from our sins and an eternity of damnation in hell will we truly want to stop the sinful behavior. The addiction or sin must be seen by the individual as a weapon that destroys the person's relationship not only with others but first and most importantly with God. The diagnosis of being HIV positive and in the early stages of AIDS was a release point for Scott. The Holy Spirit, working in God's Word and through the efforts of Scott's parents and pastors, kept Scott from missing the grace of God.

Step 3: *Replace* the sinful behavior of the addiction with deeds that are pleasing to God. Leaving behind an addiction leaves a big hole in a person's life that must be filled. In the following two passages, the apostle Paul tells us what must fill that hole in a person's life if that person is to be successful in coming out of the addiction or sinful lifestyle: "Do not conform any longer to the pattern of this world, but be transformed by the renewing of your mind. Then you will be able to test and approve what God's will is—his good, pleasing and perfect will" (Romans 12:2). "He chose us in him before the creation of the world to be holy and blameless in his sight" (Ephesians 1:4). Identify the times when you are most likely to be tempted to engage in the sinful behavior and fill that time with good and productive behavior, such as volunteering at a shelter or calling on or writing letters to prospects and delinquents at church. Try to find some useful activity that involves interaction with other people who are depending on you, and don't let them down. Scott has done this by leading Bible classes for his church and other churches in his area. He spends his own money to travel to different areas of the country to give presentations about his departure from the gay lifestyle. He also spends a great deal of time monitoring the online support group for those struggling against the temptation to practice the sin of homosexuality. These are a few examples of replacing sinful behavior with deeds that are pleasing to God.

Step 4: *Refocus* your life on God. Among numerous other passages, we find the basis for the step of refocusing your life on God in Job 11:13-16: "Yet if you devote your heart to him and stretch out your hands to him, if you put away the sin that is in your hand and allow no evil to dwell in your tent, then you will lift up your face without shame; you will stand firm and without fear. You will surely forget your trouble, recalling it only as waters gone by."

Regardless of your past, regardless of your past failures, say today, "I'm going to make a commitment to maintain God's standards." That means you agree with God about what he says about sex. God's standards have never, ever changed. God says that sex is for a man and a woman in marriage. No matter how much the gay community may spin the passages, God's truth does not and will not ever change. Society and earthly churches change in order to accommodate more and more sin; God's Word does not. By God's grace, Scott's life is now refocused on God. Scott searches God's Word daily to find strength and support that he can offer to those who, like him, are struggling every day to overcome the temptation of practicing the sin of homosexuality.

Step 5: *Reach out* to others in friendship so that they can comfort you, filling the hole left by the sinful behavior. God does not leave us without resources in overcoming temptation, including the temptation to addictive behavior such as homosexuality. Our fellow Christians are a wonderful resource that God provides to help us in our struggles to overcome temptation of all kinds. The apostle Paul wrote of that in 2 Corinthians 1:3,4: "Praise be to the God and Father of our Lord Jesus Christ, the Father of compassion and the God of all comfort, who comforts us in all our troubles, so that we can comfort those in any trouble with the comfort we ourselves have received from God." For the person struggling with homosexuality, this especially means forming new friendships with heterosexual persons of the same sex. In these new friendships, leave behind all the labels with which you have identified yourself: homo, gay, fag, lesbian, dike, etc. Due to the stigma of society, even labels such as "homosexual struggler" and "ex-gay" are not as useful as "recovering alcoholic." In the new friendships, simply be a child of God striving to live in a way that shows your love and gratitude to him. In one of his recent presentations to a group of about 60 pastors and lay leaders, Scott was asked what he calls himself. The questioner offered several options, such as recovering homosexual, ex-gay, cured gay, etc. After listening to the suggestions, Scott simply replied, "I'm not much into labels. I prefer redeemed child of God." There was a burst of applause. What an absolutely perfect response! This is exactly how every repentant sinner must view himself or herself and how every

Christian must view all other repentant sinners, no matter what sin or sins may have enslaved them in the past. If someone struggling against the sin of practicing homosexuality reaches out to you, be sure that you see that person, first and always, as a redeemed child of God.

After offering a biblical five-step program for overcoming addiction and temptations, we must note that there is no easy step-by-step formula for changing the deadly desires of homosexuality. The feelings and temptations may very well last a lifetime. However, with God's help they do not have to result in sinful behavior and they do not need to consume you. Let God fill the deep and vulnerable areas of your life left empty by the removal of the sinful behavior, and you will intimately experience his love, power, and presence.

Like the recovering alcoholic, with God's help and the help of fellow Christians reflecting Christ's love, the homosexual can lead a life that gives glory to God by daily resisting the sin of practicing homosexuality. It will be a joyful life according to the new man created in him or her by the Holy Spirit, even though the old Adam may hate and rebel against the God-pleasing way of life.

In light of all this, we must preach and teach firmly against the sin of practicing homosexuality as it becomes more and more accepted and promoted by this sinful world. There must be no doubt whatsoever concerning the sinfulness of practicing homosexuality in the minds of Christians. The false climate of respectability created for homosexuality within society and the church is the very last thing a young person with a predisposition toward homosexuality needs. He or she must be encouraged to fight the good fight of faith.

We must do all we can to help in that fight, encouraging the young person in whatever way possible not to experiment with homosexuality but to save himself or herself for heterosexual marriage. Nor can we self-righteously turn our backs on those men and women, boys and girls who are struggling against the sin of practicing homosexuality, no matter how repulsive that sin may seem to us personally. We must also be ready and willing to counsel and aid the Christian struggling against the sin of practicing homosexuality. This means that we must be approachable by anyone seeking our help. Only God knows how many of his children have had to shoulder a tremendous burden of guilt without the assistance of a fellow Christian simply because they feared being ostracized by those who could help them the most. God help us all to follow the example of our loving Savior who ate with publicans and sinners, opened his arms to all, and forgave all kinds of sins!

CHAPTER SIX

THE SUPPORT

SCOTT'S JOURNEY
Part 6: "I Never Promised You a Rose Garden"

In the preceding five sections of recalling my journey, I hope I was able to convey the roller coaster that has characterized the last 20 years of my life (from my teens to the present). At the end of the last section, I shared how God the Holy Spirit had led me to see and acknowledge my sinful lifestyle, to repent of it, to return to regular study of his complete *Word*, and to worship and participate in a church that proclaims the complete *message of God's full law and gospel*. Finally, the Holy Spirit led me to make my exodus from the fantasy land of thinking that I could live as a practicing homosexual and as a forgiven child of God. All praise be to God *for that!*

And to be sure, wouldn't my journey have been much happier, sort of like a Hallmark movie, if I had been able to say that I just woke up one morning with the burning desire to repent, without contracting HIV and AIDS? Or that after years of searching, my parents or pastor finally found the right combination of words or Bible passages to effect that change? But I have come to look at things this way: Sure, I have a terminal illness. But life here on earth, in and of itself, is a terminal illness. If I hadn't hit rock bottom by way of contracting HIV and the Holy Spirit hadn't used that to help snap me out of that perpetual cycle of sin, bringing me to repentance, I may have lived a few extra years here on earth. But I would hate to think about where I would then be spending eternity. Not a pleasant thought! So I would say that my journey is one with a very happy ending!

I will pick up with the teaser that ended chapter 5. I alluded to the fact that I never did wake up one day with a sudden attraction for women. If that had occurred, this journey of mine would have an even happier ending; but, regrettably, that isn't the case. However, in my opinion, *that's okay too! I firmly agree with Pastor Starr in that there are distinctive similarities between the sin of practicing homosexuality and other addictive sins. Would you belittle a recovering alcoholic who hasn't had a drink in four years just because he or she still has to struggle against that temptation every day? No, of course not; you could continue to rejoice with that individual because that person has managed to continue to* resist temptation! *I believe it is the same way with some recovering homosexuals like me. (Although I also agree with Pastor Starr that there is no benefit in officially giving myself that label.)*

Do not get me wrong though. I continue to pray daily that this temptation might be completely removed from me at some point. I find great comfort in the fact that our God is truly an awesome God and that all things are possible with God! As Jesus reminds all of us in Mark 10:27, "With man this is impossible, but not with God; all things are possible with God."

But just as a recovering alcoholic has to make some drastic changes in his or her life, so too have I. Unfortunately, I had to make a clean break from socializing with a number of close friends from my days of living in unrepentant sin. Some might question that, perhaps saying, "Well, you could have continued to see them and then tried to use your connections and friendship with them to share God's Word and be a witness to them." I did offer explicit explanations to these friends as to why I no longer felt like I could socialize with them. The places we had always socialized as friends were gay establishments: bars, clubs, restaurants, etc. God promises to help us resist temptation, but we also have to flee from temptation (1 Corinthians 6:18). If I were to go back to a gay bar or restaurant with these friends, I would be placing myself right back in the lap of temptation. It would be tantamount to a newly recovering alcoholic hanging out in a bar!

Finally, I'd like to offer a piece of my own advice to those who have a family member or friend who has recently proclaimed himself or herself to be a homosexual. It is simply this: Do not burn your bridges with that person! *After looking back at where I've personally been, I recognize how true the statement is,* Love the sinner, but hate the sin. *You do need to share God's law, but you need to proclaim it with sincere love and concern for the individual. Be cognizant of your approach. Whether you write a letter to this person or sit down with him or her, you might be inclined to rattle off in one session every Bible passage that Pastor Starr has shared, especially those that speak of God's condemnation of homosexuality. You may view your approach as an act of tough Christian love for that individual. But if that's your entire message and approach, it would be tantamount not only to setting fire to the bridge (your relationship with that person), but it would also be like dousing it with gasoline before setting fire to it. Again, I'm not saying he or she shouldn't hear God's law from you. But be very careful to avoid placing yourself in a position where it seems you are standing atop the mountain and doing nothing but casting fire and brimstone down upon this individual. Paul has some wonderful and inspired advice for all of us in this regard: "Brothers, if someone is caught in a sin, you who are spiritual should restore him gently. But watch yourself, or you also may be tempted. Carry each other's burdens, and in this way you will fulfill the law of Christ" (Galatians 6:1,2).*

As I look back on my own life, I wonder what might have happened if a relative or close friend from my church had made the effort to maintain some sort of relationship or contact with me over the years after I came out. There actually were a couple of other times of turmoil and crisis in my life (before contracting HIV and losing my career), when I may have turned back to them for support instead of turning to other gay friends. So even if you feel your friend or loved one has been the one to sever ties with you, make every attempt to stay in touch. Periodically call, e-mail, or send notes and cards, if for no other reason than to say, "I still care about you"; "Just checking in"; "Miss you"; etc. Remember the book that my dad sent to me? At the time I never gave serious consideration to it, but I never actually threw it out either. Years later I would turn to it for help. Never discount the small gestures; they might later pay off with huge dividends!

I would like to leave you with two passages from God's Word that have held true for me. I pray they will also hold true for you, your loved one, or a friend who might currently be struggling with the temptation of homosexuality or living as an unrepentant homosexual: "Train a child in the way he should go, and when he is old he will not turn from it" (Proverbs 22:6); "Surely I am with you always, to the very end of the age" (Matthew 28:20).

—Scott Barefoot, redeemed child of God

77

THE SUPPORT

In the film *Steel Magnolias,* the story is told of a young man who sits down with his parents and with a tragic tone tells them solemnly, "Mom, Dad, I want to tell you I have terminal brain cancer."

The parents are stunned, shocked. There is silence.

The son continues, "Just kidding. I'm fine. But I do want to tell you I'm gay."[10]

That's quite a way to come out! The strategy, of course, was to make the parents think something fatal was happening to their son so that in comparison his homosexuality wouldn't seem so bad. In the movie, it worked. Does it in real life? Most people realize that the announcement of their sexual preference will create a shock in their family.

Barbara Johnson experienced that shock herself one day. She is a woman whose husband died at an early age and who lost a son in the Vietnam War. Then she discovered that her other son was gay. In her book *Where Does a Mother Go to Resign?* (Bethany House, 1979), she describes her anguish. "Flashing in my mind was this wonderful son who was so bubbly and happy—such a joy to have around. Thinking of him entwined with some other male brought heaves of heavy sobbing from deep wounds of agony." Her book provides encouragement and hope from a Christian perspective to those who are coping with a loved one engaged in homosexual behavior. It is also an excellent read for those who are struggling with the temptation to engage in homosexual behavior.

GIVING SUPPORT

First of all, know that neither this book nor any book you read on the subject will give you all the right answers for every situation in dealing with homosexuality. There is no one right thing to say that will bring about the change you desire in yourself or in someone else. Only the Holy Spirit can bring about repentance for righteousness. Remember also that you cannot change someone else; you can only change yourself, with the help of the Holy Spirit. I pray that as you support someone struggling with homosexuality, you will find the proper balance between showing love and openness to the person and maintaining your firm and unwavering stand on what God says about this sin. Scott gave wise encouragement along these lines, emphasizing the importance of maintaining contact with the person without condoning the sinful lifestyle and being patient while constantly praying for the person.

Heterosexual Christians are often shocked and stunned when they learn that a relative or friend is struggling with the sin of practicing homosexuality. They do not know how to react. Early in my ministry, I felt that way when a young gay man asked me, "Would my partner and I be welcome in your church?" At first I felt woefully unprepared to deal with that question and situation. I replied, "Everyone is welcome at our church. But the members of our church are repentant sinners who strive to not live in sin." Of course, the problem was that the young gay couple did not believe they were living in sin.

It was not until sometime later that I realized my seminary training had prepared me very well for dealing with that situation. No, we had not spent much time at all talking about how to deal with homosexuals, but we had spent all our time learning how to deal with sinners. That was the real preparation that was needed. Every one of our pastors has received that preparation. Every teacher in our Lutheran elementary schools has received the preparation. Every Christian who reads and studies the Bible has too. The apostle Paul reminds us of how we are to feel toward and deal with the sinner, including anyone struggling with or trapped in the sin of practicing homosexuality. "God did not appoint us to suffer wrath but to receive salvation through our Lord Jesus Christ. He died for us so that, whether we are awake or asleep, we may live together with him. Therefore encourage one another and build each other up, just as in fact you are doing" (1 Thessalonians 5:9-11). God wants us to see every sinner, including the homosexual, as someone for whom Jesus suffered and died. God does not want the homosexual to continue in his or her sin, to die, and to suffer wrath. So, God wants us to encourage the homosexual to repent, and God wants us to build up the homosexual in faith and Christian living.

Realize that most often today the homosexual will not feel a need to change his or her behavior until the person has experienced a crisis of some sort. The law of God is still written in the heart of natural man. Although it condemns the practice of homosexuality as unnatural, that natural law is being squelched and silenced more and more in the hearts of all people, not just those who are tempted with same-sex desires. Unless you have been living under a rock for the last several decades, you know that there has been a tremendous surge of interest in affirming homosexuality in every area of our society. The homosexual agenda is at the heart of redefining marriage in our country. It's at the heart of legislation against discrimination and "hate speech." It's at the heart of the elevation of the gay lifestyle in the media and education. It is enjoying great success on many fronts. There is now tolerance, acceptance, and even promotion of homosexuality among national churches. These churches that refuse to proclaim the sinfulness of homosexuality are doing horrendous damage to souls by calling evil good and good evil. Unless they repent, they will not escape God's wrath, as he declares in Isaiah 5:20: "Woe to those who call evil good and good evil, who put darkness for light and light for darkness, who put bitter for sweet and sweet for bitter."

Historically, Christians exhibit one of two reactions to the success of the gay agenda in our society. Some respond with tolerance and accept the lie that God made homosexuals that way so it must be all right. Others respond by condemning and excluding homosexuals with disdain and hostility.

As we have tried to show throughout this book, what is called for—what the Bible calls for—is a balance between condemnation and compassion. Both condemnation and compassion are essential elements of biblical love. That's what every homosexual needs; that's what every sinner needs.

As redeemed children of God, we must never compromise concerning what the Bible says about the sin of homosexuality. We are not showing love and compassion to a person struggling with homosexuality or to a person stubbornly living the gay lifestyle if we let that person think it is permissible to change or ignore what God so clearly says about the sin. We dare not join in the defiant rebellion against God, his creation, and his will, which is at the heart of the agenda pushed by proponents of homosexuality, whether they realize it or not.

As you deal with a family member or friend who is struggling with the temptation of practicing homosexuality or who is stubbornly trapped in the sin, realize that there is likely going to be a confrontation. Your attitude will greatly affect the outcome of that confrontation. Let your loving and concerned heart be blatantly evident as you affirm God's condemnation of the sin of homosexuality. Be positively certain that the person knows your goal is not to bring damnation on him or her. You are sharing God's Word with the person so that the Holy Spirit can touch the person's heart and mind. Make sure the person knows that God and you want the person to repent, to turn from the sin, and to find forgiveness, strength, and comfort in the only hope of salvation for all sinners—our Lord Jesus Christ.

Approach the person who is struggling with the temptation of practicing homosexuality or who is stubbornly trapped in the sin with these facts firmly established in your own heart and mind:

- Homosexuals need salvation.

- Homosexuals do not need healing—homosexuality is not a disease.

- Homosexuals need forgiveness, because homosexuality is a sin.

The apostle Paul wrote of this necessary balance between condemnation and compassion in 1 Corinthians 6:9-11:

> Do you not know that the wicked will not inherit the kingdom of God? Do not be deceived: Neither the sexually immoral nor idolaters nor adulterers nor male prostitutes nor homosexual offenders nor thieves nor the greedy nor drunkards nor slanderers nor swindlers will inherit the kingdom of God. And that is what some of you were. But you were washed, you were sanctified, you were justified

in the name of the Lord Jesus Christ and by the Spirit of our God.

Right after asserting that homosexuals, among many other unrepentant sinners, will not inherit the kingdom of God but instead be separated from God for all eternity, Paul holds out the glorious hope, comfort, and life-changing power of the gospel. "But you were washed, you were sanctified, you were justified in the name of the Lord Jesus Christ and by the Spirit of our God." What encouragement and hope there is in Paul's matter-of-fact statement for people like Scott, who struggle daily against the temptation of practicing homosexuality, and for all of us sinners: "And that is what some of you were." Change for the homosexual is possible, achievable, and documented.

But God may use a crisis to get the attention of the person who is struggling with the temptation of practicing homosexuality or is stubbornly trapped in the sin and give friends, family members, and pastors an opportunity to serve the person with the whole Word of God. Scott mentioned the crisis of his diagnosis with HIV and losing his chosen career. He also mentioned turmoil and crisis in his life prior to hitting rock bottom with the HIV diagnosis and the job loss. However, even if the person is displaying a stubborn attitude and won't change his or her behavior, take it as a compliment if the person has confided in you about his or her desires. You have a relationship that the person feels he or she can trust. You have an open door and the opportunity to work with the person, sharing the powerful Word of God, which alone can bring about the desire and strength to change.

The spiritual condition of the person who believes that he or she can be a Christian while pursuing the gay lifestyle, a condition that Scott was in for several years, is heartrending. The apostle Paul described such people almost two thousand years ago by inspiration of the Holy Spirit:

> Then we will no longer be infants, tossed back and forth by the waves, and blown here and there by every wind of teaching and by the cunning and craftiness of men in their deceitful scheming. Instead, speaking the truth in

love, we will in all things grow up into him who is the Head, that is, Christ. From him the whole body, joined and held together by every supporting ligament, grows and builds itself up in love, as each part does its work. (Ephesians 4:14-16)

They truly are "infants, tossed back and forth by the waves, and blown here and there by every wind of teaching and by the cunning and craftiness of men in their deceitful scheming." "Christian" proponents of homosexuality have not been particularly clever in their twisting and spinning of God's clear Word to try to excuse their sin. Most of their misinterpretations are mere smoke screens that quickly dissipate when one approaches the passage with humility and examines it in its context and takes its clear and obvious meaning. Their misinterpretations are warped and irrational but are believed because people want to believe the lie. The lie justifies their sin. They don't want to see what God says because it would mean they are wrong. As it has been said, there is none so blind as he who will not see.

We must keep speaking the truth in love. But that can be difficult, especially when you know that the hearer will likely be offended and will not want to hear the truth. However, you must share the Word of God—the law and the gospel—for only God's Word has the power to touch individual hearts.

It is often cited by homosexual proponents that Jesus said nothing about homosexuality. While we cannot point to a specific passage in which Jesus mentioned homosexuality, he certainly taught and upheld God's natural plan for human beings as male and female. Jesus also gave us a wonderful example to follow in dealing with a person caught in sin, including the sin of homosexuality. You may wish to read the account of Jesus dealing with the woman at the well in Samaria in John 4:1-42. From this account we can learn how Jesus dealt with a person trapped in a sinful lifestyle.

It was remarkable that Jesus spoke with this woman at all. In fact, he went out of his way to speak with her and sent his disciples away for a time so that he could speak with her alone. Jesus truly sought her out and made time for her. This was unusual because

Jews did not associate with Samaritans for religious and racist reasons. For a Jewish man, a rabbi no less, speaking with a Samaritan woman was unheard of. In the minds of some on both sides of the issue of homosexuality, a Christian talking with a homosexual would be just as astonishing.

Jesus also treated this woman, who had and was still living a scandalously sinful lifestyle, with respect. He accepted her as a person, but he did not accept her sin. He listened to her. He showed that he cared about her, offering her "living water." In the same way, we need to treat a person trapped in homosexuality with respect and accept the person but not the sinful behavior. Remember, we are all sinners. We must also show that we care about the person. Many homosexuals feel that no one in the straight world cares about them. For extended periods of time many have lived in shame, loneliness, isolation, and fear that no other Christian could possibly have the feelings they have, that no other Christian could possibly be struggling with the same temptations. They feel no straight person can really handle the truth about a homosexual. They have found relief in the world of the homosexual; they need to know they can find caring people in the straight world too.

Also remember that Jesus spoke confidentially with the woman at the well. It was no accident that he sent his disciples away so that he could have a private conversation with this woman. We need to keep that in mind when dealing with a fellow sinner. This is certainly true when talking with a homosexual about his or her sin. Jesus and the woman had an honest and open exchange of questions and answers. This is also important when dealing with a homosexual. You may need time to sort out your own feelings regarding this news that is probably surprising and certainly disappointing. If so, take the time, but ask for permission to speak with the person again soon. You need to get to the point where you, like Jesus, can focus on the person's problems rather than on your own adverse reaction. At this point, don't condemn if the person is seeking help or just seeing if you can be trusted. Jesus didn't condemn the woman for her sinful lifestyle but let her know he knew of it. She knew it was wrong; that's why she so quickly changed the subject. The homosexual knows the behavior is wrong; he or she is looking to see if you can be trusted to help. Ask God to help you be the answer to that person's prayer.

The spiritual condition of the woman at the well is remarkably similar to that of a person who believes that he or she can continue to live the gay lifestyle with God's blessing. Though the woman had not been properly instructed, she knew some of the truth. She was trapped in a sinful lifestyle. The person seeking your help may very well believe some of God's truth, but may have been misled by false teachers and lies about homosexuality. He or she is trapped in a sinful lifestyle. But there is hope. There is always hope with Jesus and his Word.

Finally, notice the all-important attitude with which Jesus approached this woman living a sinful lifestyle. Jesus lovingly shared the truth with the Samaritan woman. He brought her sin to light, but he also assured her of forgiveness. She responded with Spirit-worked faith. When you have the opportunity to share God's Word with a struggling homosexual, you may witness the same result. Or you may experience defensiveness, rejection, and ridicule. You may be tempted to fire back at the person, and a war of words could escalate into a broken relationship with no more opportunities to share the Word of Truth. So be ready. You may be hurt. What the person says in retaliation may not be fair. You, however, need to respond with questions that will keep the lines of communication open. Ask, "Why do you say that?" or "Why do you think that?" Keep communication open. Scott's father did exactly that over the decade that his son was wallowing in the sin of living the gay lifestyle. Then, when Scott had been prepared for the truth and a return to the Lord by the Holy Spirit, the door was open and Scott could pick up the book his father had sent him and begin his Spirit-led exodus from the gay lifestyle.

Of course, your efforts may not yield your desired results immediately. Remember, Scott's father waited over a decade for his prayers for his son to be answered. If the person who has revealed his or her homosexuality to you shows no sign of wanting to change, if the person insists that he or she cannot change and that you just have to accept the person the way he or she is, you must stand firmly on God's Word. You cannot and dare not give the impression that the person's choice of behavior is acceptable to God or to you. If there is no repentance, then you cannot share the gospel of forgiveness. However, you can keep the door open by saying something like this: "As a Christian, this must be a very difficult struggle for you. You know the truth, but you can't find the strength to act on it yet. But know this: God loves you and I love you. God forgives, and he wants you to receive his forgiveness. God is powerful, and he wants to give you the strength to change. I know change is possible with God."

You may recall from chapter 5 that the first step in overcoming an addictive temptation is to reveal it to God and to others who can assist in overcoming that temptation. This is a huge step—and not natural for our sinful nature. It has been unnatural since our first parents committed the first sin. In Genesis 3:8-10 we read of the sinful but all too natural response of people when their sin is about to be revealed: "Then the man and his wife heard the sound of the LORD God as he was walking in the garden in the cool of the day, and they hid from the LORD God among the trees of the garden. But the LORD God called to the man, 'Where are you?' He answered, 'I heard you in the garden, and I was afraid because I was naked; so I hid.'" Many Christians who struggle with homosexuality also must constantly deal with shame and guilt. They want to hide from God, but they know they cannot. They have been or are hiding from all those who can help them, because they fear rejection. They need to come out in the open to someone and receive the help that God offers. Study God's Word, pray, and live your life in such a way that you might be that someone to a person who needs you.

If someone has opened up to you about their deadly desires for homosexual behavior, you are the tool in God's hand to help that person. Will you always know the right words to say? No. But if you view the person as a precious blood-bought soul for whom our Savior suffered and died, God will give you the right words to say as the Holy Spirit helps you grow in love, understanding, and compassion for the person. The Lord bless your work, your caring, and your sharing.

A RECOVERY PLAN
FOR THE HOMOSEXUAL[11]

If you want to overcome deadly desires for homosexual behavior, here is a simple recovery plan you can begin using right away. Be sure to answer each question fully and honestly.

1. What event or circumstances motivated your decision to repent of homosexuality?

2. What specifically will you need to repent of (turn from)? (Examples: use of pornography, ongoing relationship, anonymous sexual encounters, Internet porn, phone sex, etc.) Be specific and honest.

3. List any ways your sexual behavior has affected you physically.

4. List any ways your sexual behavior has affected you mentally or emotionally. (Examples: mental images, depression, loss of self-respect, fear, distraction, etc.)

5. List any ways your sexual behavior has affected you spiritually. (Examples: loss of intimacy with God, spiritual attack, withdrawal from fellowship, etc.)

6. Describe what your life will be like five years from now if you don't stop this behavior. (Include a description of how this behavior will affect your marriage, job, spiritual life, relationships, and view of yourself.)

7. You just described what your life will be like if you continue in this behavior. Is this acceptable to you? Why or why not?

If you do not have a devotional life, begin reading a book of the Bible today. Here are some suggested books with which to begin: gospel of John, Romans, Ephesians, James, Proverbs.

8. The book of the Bible I will begin reading today is:
_____.

After reading a chapter of the Bible, spend some time in prayer. You may wish to ask God to help you with these and your own specific requests:

a. I want intimacy with God.

b. I want to become the sort of man/woman I can honestly respect.

c. I'm tired of lying, hiding, and covering up.

d. I want peace of mind.

e. I don't want to be a part of the world's problems.

It is absolutely necessary for you to get and keep structure in your life. You have to break out of your sinful behavioral pattern. You need to replace it with something else. Structure in your life, where you make yourself responsible to yourself and to others, is one of the keys to a successful lifestyle change. Consider the following as a plan for your life, for the rest of your life.

Scripture Reading and Prayer 20 minutes daily

Support Group 90 minutes weekly

(You may wish to contact Scott Barefoot for information on the online group he monitors. You can find Scott on Facebook. Or it can be a general men's or women's accountability group. It needs to be a group that encourages participants to stay on course and one in which you can be honest about your struggles and goals.)

Recreation 2 hours twice monthly

(Plan something enjoyable and fun with friends, preferably of both genders.)

Pastoral Care 30 minutes monthly

(Ask for a half hour of your pastor's time each month to check in with him on your progress, your struggles, and for any prayers or insight he may have to share.)

Therapy 1 hour weekly

(You may wish to contact Wisconsin Lutheran Child and Family Service at 888-685-9522 for help in this area.)

To be the person you want to be, you will need to maintain sexual integrity. Since you may have been living a lifestyle that was anything but that, this will not be easy. Habits are hard to break, but they can be broken, and new ones, good habits, can replace them. Again, structure and accountability will help you accomplish this. Each week, maybe each day for awhile, ask yourself and have a trusted friend ask you these questions:

1. Did you use pornography in any form?

2. Did you put yourself in a position where you would have been likely to use it?

3. Did you make some kind of social plans this week with friends who will help you maintain proper behavior?

4. Did you keep those plans?

5. Have you answered these questions honestly?[12]

MOTTO: "I can do everything through him who gives me strength" (Philippians 4:13).

"A Recovery Plan for a Homosexual" is adapted from:
Desires in Conflict
Copyright © 1991 by Joe Dallas (revised 2003)
Published by Harvest House Publishers
Eugene, Oregon 97402
www.harvesthousepublishers.com

ENDNOTES

1. Michael O'Shea, *Parade,* October 12, 2008, p. 20.

2. Joe Dallas, *Desires in Conflict: Hope for Men Who Struggle With Sexual Identity* (Eugene: Harvest House Publishers, 2003), p. 7.

3. *Ibid.,* p. 97.

4. Virginia Mollenkott and Letha Scanzoni, *Is the Homosexual My Neighbor?* (San Francisco: HarperCollins, 1978), pp. 57,58.

5. Thomas Schmidt, *Straight & Narrow? Compassion and Clarity in the Homosexual Debate* (Downers Grove: Intervarsity Press, 1995), pp. 88,89.

6. John Boswell, *Christianity, Social Tolerance and Homosexuality* (Chicago: University of Chicago Press, 1978), p. 109.

7. Troy Perry and Thomas Swicegood, *Don't Be Afraid Anymore: The Story of Reverend Troy Perry and the Metropolitan Community Churches* (New York: St. Martin's Press, 1990), p. 341.

8. Jeffrey Satinover, *Homosexuality and the Politics of Truth* (Grand Rapids: Baker Book House, 1996), p. 49.

9. *Ibid.,* p. 51.

10. Dallas, *Desires in Conflict,* p. 229.

11. *Ibid.,* pp. 87-90.

12. *Ibid.,* p. 156.